OpenOffice 3.4
Volume IV: Impress

quantum scientific publishing

OpenOffice 3.4
Volume IV: Impress

CHRISTOPHER N. CAIN

RILEY W. WALKER

quantum scientific publishing

OpenOffice 3.4
Volume IV: Impress

ISBN-13: 978-1480224384
ISBN-10: 1480224383

Published by quantum scientific publishing

Pittsburgh, PA | Copyright © 2012

Cover design by Scott Sheariss

Table of Contents

Unit Three

Appendix

Unit One

Section 1.1 – Introduction to OpenOffice Impress

Section Objective:

- Learn how to get started in OpenOffice Impress.

Introduction

Welcome to OpenOffice Impress. Impress is a powerful multimedia presentation tool, and is just one of six applications found within the Apache OpenOffice Suite 3.4. If not already installed, download the latest version of the Apache OpenOffice Suite from the www.openoffice.org website. When the page loads, click "I want to download OpenOffice" to be directed to the download page. Follow the instructions to complete the download.

This book begins by introducing the basic features and layout of Impress, and then progresses to more complex functions and operations. At the end of each section, there are questions which test readers' understanding of the application. Use these questions, as well as the steps provided in this book, to learn many different tasks which can be accomplished in OpenOffice Impress.

OpenOffice Impress

OpenOffice Impress is an application that allows users to create slideshows that include text, graphics, sound, video, and animations. This section will provide users with some terms that will be encountered when working with this application. Some of the terms below are parts of the Impress application, while others are objects and multimedia that can be added to a presentation.

- **Animations** – Animations are a visual or sound effect accompanying any text or graphics on the presentation slide.

- **ClipArt** – ClipArt is a picture that can be added to a presentation. Users can access the ClipArt that OpenOffice provides in the Gallery, or different pictures can be uploaded and used.

- **Master** – A Master contains formatting and design elements common to every slide in a presentation.

- **Objects** – An Object is an item or graphic imported from another source such as a scanned image. A piece of uploaded ClipArt is an example of an object.

- **Presentation** – A Presentation is a file containing a collection of slides.

- **Slide Show** – A Slide Show is a presentation of the Impress slides. There are a variety of mediums that can be used to show the slide show.

- **Template** – A Template contains default slide settings. Impress provides a library of templates as well as templates that can be created by the user.

- **Transitions** – A Transition is the effect that takes place when advancing from one slide to another.

- **Wizard** – A Wizard is a step-by-step guide for completing a task in Impress.

Opening Impress

To open Impress, go to the **Start** menu and select **All Programs** → **OpenOffice.org 3.4** → **OpenOffice Impress**.

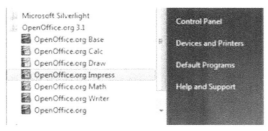

Figure 1

A blank Impress presentation will appear on the screen.

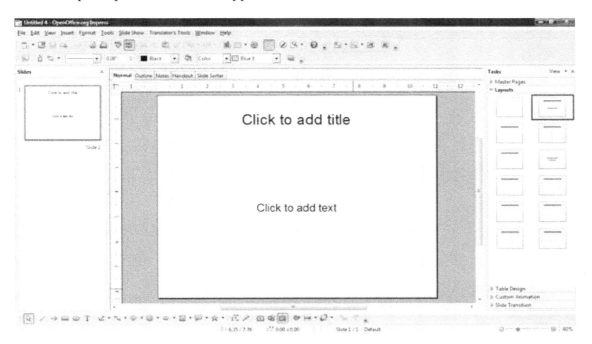

Figure 2

Growth & Assessment

1. What is ClipArt?

2. What is a Wizard?

3. Users can access the ClipArt that OpenOffice provides in the Gallery, or different pictures can be uploaded and used.

   a. TRUE

   b. FALSE

4. What is a Master?

Section 1.2 – Impress Features

Section Objective:

- Learn how to get started with OpenOffice Impress by identifying the features on the application window.

Features on the Application Window

When OpenOffice Impress is opened, users will notice that there are many differences between the Impress application window, and others that users may be familiar with, such as Microsoft PowerPoint.

Figure 1

In Impress, there are a series of pull-down menus and toolbars that contain all of the tools available. Clicking on one of the Menu Bar options will cause the drop-down menus to open and the tools within them will be displayed.

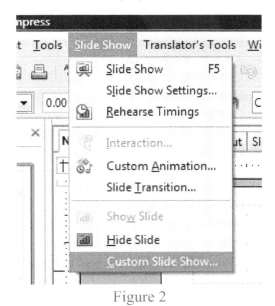

Figure 2

Tools for each command tab are divided into groups (Duplicate Slide, Links, and Text tools in Impress's Insert menu). Some tools on the Menu Bar's drop-down menus are context-sensitive, displaying only when a particular feature is being used. For example, when a graphic is inserted into an Impress slide and is selected, the **Interactions...** menu item will be available under the **Slide Show** menu.

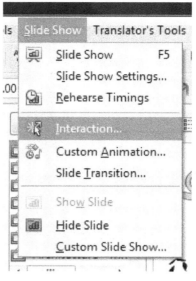

Figure 3

Many of the tools used in Impress have dialog boxes that are associated with them. These dialog boxes provide the user with additional options. For example, if a user decides to format a slide's design using the **Format** menu, Impress will display a dialog box that allows the user to choose the specifics of the design.

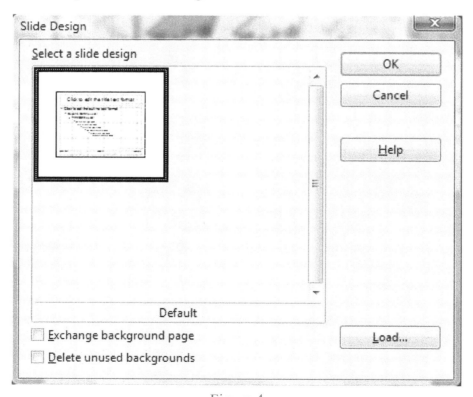

Figure 4

Impress has also created shortcut icons for many of the most commonly used tools in the application.

Figure 5

Note – To display the name of a tool, position the cursor over the icon and the tool's name will automatically appear on the screen.

Figure 6

Use the tools that are found on the Toolbar by clicking the icon with the left mouse button. For example, clicking on the **Table** toolbar button will cause the **Insert Table** dialog box to appear.

Figure 7

Growth & Assessment

1. The tools on the toolbar can be accessed by clicking their icons with the left mouse button.

    a. TRUE

    b. FALSE

2. How would a user display the name of a tool?

3. Impress has created shortcut icons for many of the most commonly used tools in the application.

    a. TRUE

    b. FALSE

Section 1.3 – Changing Slide Size and Orientation

Section Objectives:

- Learn how to change the size of a slide.

- Learn how to change the orientation of a slide.

Changing Slide Size and Orientation

OpenOffice Impress allows users to change the slide's size and orientation. Changing the orientation is important when users need to accommodate a particular style or illustration within a slide. This section will outline how users can change the height and width of a slide, as well as change a slide's orientation to better display the objects within it.

Steps for Changing Slide Size:

Step 1: Click **Format**, located on the Menu Bar.

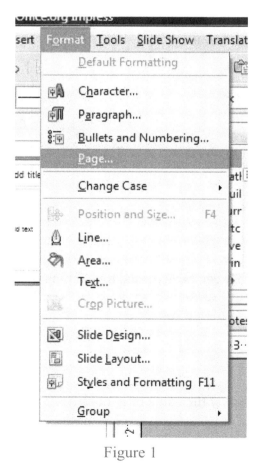

Figure 1

Step 2: From the Format drop-down menu, select **Page…**. The **Page Setup** dialog box will appear.

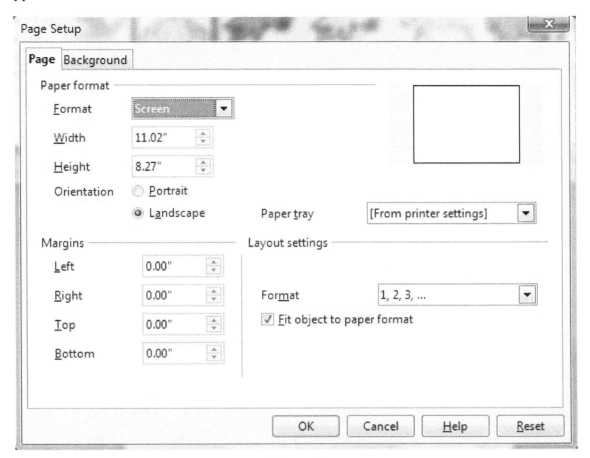

Figure 2

Step 3: Type the preferred slide width and height in the appropriate textboxes.

Figure 3

Step 4: Click **OK**. The slides will automatically resize based on the dimensions entered in **Step 3**.

Figure 4

Steps for Changing Slide Orientation:

OpenOffice Impress provides users with two different orientations to use for a slide. The orientations are **Portrait** (vertical) and **Landscape** (horizontal). In this exercise, change the orientation of the slide from **Landscape**, which is the default, to **Portrait**.

Step 1: Click **Format**, located on the Menu Bar.

Step 2: From the Format drop-down menu, select **Page...**. The **Page Setup** dialog box will appear.

Step 3: Click on the **Portrait** radio button to change the orientation.

Step 4: Click **OK**. The orientation will be applied to the slide.

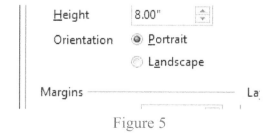

Figure 5

Note – The orientation can be changed back to Landscape by going through the steps above and selecting the Landscape radio button when the Page Setup dialog box appears.

Growth & Assessment

1. Side size and orientation are permanent in Impress.

   a. TRUE

   b. FALSE

2. What is Portrait orientation also referred to?

3. Landscape is also known as horizontal orientation.

   a. TRUE

   b. FALSE

4. Why is the ability to change a slide's orientation important?

Section 1.4 – Editing Slides

Section Objective:

- Learn ways to edit a slide in Impress.

Editing Slides

Once a slide has been created in OpenOffice Impress, users may want to edit the slide by adding, moving, or deleting text. This section will navigate the user through the necessary steps to edit and move text with the Cut and Copy techniques. Before following the steps below, open Impress and enter text into the Title slide that appears. Do this by clicking inside the Title textbox and typing the preferred text. Once this has been done, follow the steps below to learn how to move text by using the Cut technique.

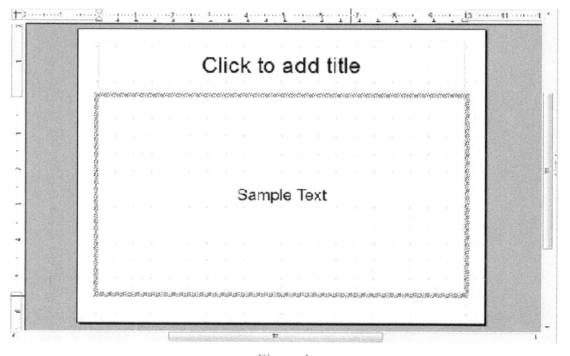

Figure 1

Cutting text from the slide will remove the text from the page and move it to the clipboard. The text can then be pasted back into the slide where it is needed. The following steps outline this process.

Step 1: Highlight the text entered into the Title textbox.

Figure 2

Step 2: Click **Edit**, located on the Menu Bar.

Step 3: From the Edit drop-down menu, select **Cut**.

> **Note** – The keyboard shortcut **CTRL + X** will also cut the text from the slide.

| Text

Figure 3

Step 4: Place the insertion point in the desired position within the textbox.

Step 5: Go back into the **Edit** drop-down menu and click **Paste**.

> **Note** – The keyboard shortcut **CTRL + V** will also paste the text back into the slide.

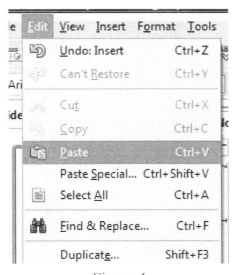

Figure 4

Text Sample

Figure 5

The Copy Technique

To duplicate portions of text within the slide, use the **Copy** technique. When copying portions of the text, the text will be placed into the Clipboard just as it was when using the Cut technique; however, the original text will not be removed from the slide. The steps below outline this process.

Step 1: Open Impress and enter text into the Title textbox.

Step 2: Highlight a portion of the text.

Step 3: Click **Edit**, located on the Menu Bar.

Step 4: From the Edit drop-down menu, select **Copy**. The text will be moved to the Clipboard and remain in its original position.

> **Note** – The keyboard shortcut **CTRL + C** will also copy the text from the slide.

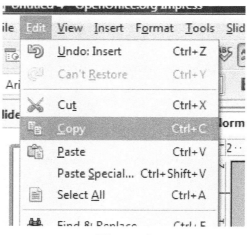

Figure 6

Step 5: Place the insertion point in the desired position within the textbox.

Step 6: Go back into the **Edit** drop-down menu and click **Paste**. The copied text will be placed back into the slide with the original text.

Text Sample Text

Figure 7

Growth & Assessment

1. What is the keyboard shortcut to Cut?

2. Text cannot be cut or copied.

    a. TRUE

    b. FALSE

3. What is the keyboard shortcut to Paste?

Section 1.5 – Slide Views in Impress

Section Objective:

- Learn about different slide views available in Impress.

Slide Views Available in Impress

OpenOffice Impress provides users with a variety of views. Depending on the user's preference, it can be helpful to work on the presentation from a different view. A user can access the available views Impress has to offer from the **View** drop-down menu, which is located on the Menu Bar. Impress also allows users to switch between views by selecting the tabs at the top of the presentation window. Below is a list of the available views provided by OpenOffice Impress.

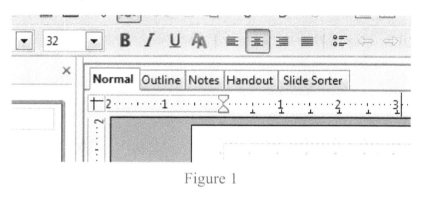

Figure 1

Available Views:

- **Normal view** – Normal view is the main editing view. Here, the user can write and design the presentation.

- **Slide Sorter view** – Slide Sorter view is a view of the slides in thumbnail form.

- **Notes view** – Impress allows the user to type notes in the **Notes** pane, which is located just below the Slide pane in Normal view.

- **Slide Show view** – Use Slide Show view to deliver the presentation to the audience.

- **Outline view** – The Outline view contains all of the slides of the presentation in their numbered sequence. Only the text in each slide is shown.

- **Handout view** – This view is for setting up the layout of the slide for a printed handout. Layout contains five choices: one, two, three, four, and six slides per page.

Growth & Assessment

1. What is the normal view?

2. How many choices does the Handout view offer?

3. A user can access the available views Impress has to offer from the View drop-down menu, located on the Menu Bar.

   a. TRUE

   b. FALSE

4. What does the Notes view allow the user to do?

Section 1.6 – Creating Custom Tab Stops

Section Objective:

- Learn how to create custom tab stops on the horizontal ruler.

Creating Custom Tab Stops

In OpenOffice Impress, another way to set up the slides for a presentation is to create tabs for the text added to the slides. There are four different types of tabs that are available in Impress which are: *Left*, *Right*, *Center*, and *Decimal*. Left justified is the default tab type in Impress, but the other options are all available in the **Paragraph** dialog box. Further explanation of the different types of tab stops is covered later in this section.

The **Ruler** option is an easy way to set and adjust tabs in a slide. The Ruler option allows the user to set, move, delete, or change tabs while working on a slide. To work with the Ruler, the user needs to have it displayed. To display the Ruler, select **View** from the Menu Bar. From the View drop-down menu, make sure that there is a check next to **Ruler**. Once Ruler is checked, the horizontal Ruler will appear.

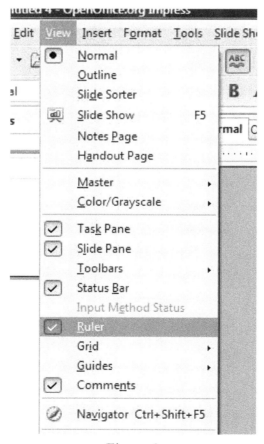

Figure 1

18

Creating Left Justified Tab Stops

The steps below outline how to create, modify, and delete left justified tab stops using the horizontal ruler.

Steps for Creating a Custom Tab Stop:

Step 1: Using the left mouse button, click anywhere within the slide where text can be added.

Step 2: On the Ruler, click at the 2 inch mark. A new left justified tab icon will appear on the ruler. The custom tab stop will be created and the user can begin adding text.

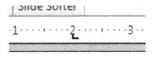

Figure 2

Steps for Modifying a Custom Tab Stop:

Step 1: Using the same slide as above, click and hold the tab previously created on the horizontal Ruler.

Step 2: Drag the tab to the 3 inch mark and release the left mouse button. The tab will move to the new location.

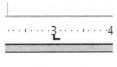

Figure 3

Steps for Deleting a Custom Tab Stop:

Step 1: Click and hold the left justified tab previously created in the steps above.

Step 2: Drag the tab into the slides area of the screen and release the left mouse button. The tab will no longer appear in the ruler.

Creating Different Types of Tab Stops

As stated above, OpenOffice Impress allows users to create four different types of tab stops. The steps above covered how to create, modify, and delete left justified tab stops. To create *Right*, *Centered*, and *Decimal* tab stops, follow the steps below.

Step 1: Using the left mouse button, click anywhere text can be added within the slide.

Step 2: Click **Format**, located on the Menu Bar.

Step 3: From the Format drop-down menu, select **Paragraph…**. The **Paragraph** dialog box will appear.

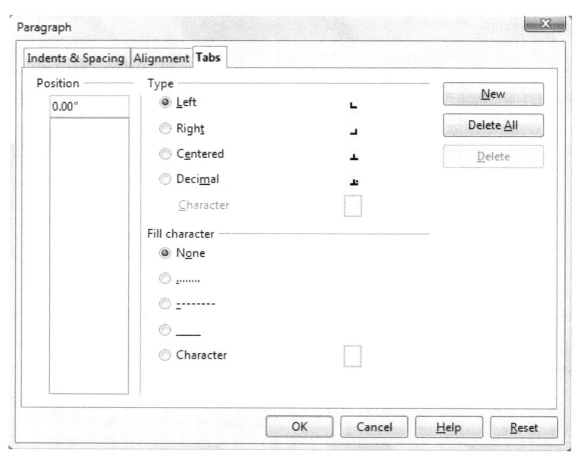

Figure 4

Step 4: Select the **Tabs** tab along the top of the Paragraph dialog box.

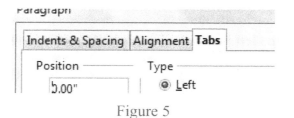

Figure 5

Step 5: From the **Tabs** window, click the radio button next to the preferred tab type (*Left, Right, Center,* or *Decimal*).

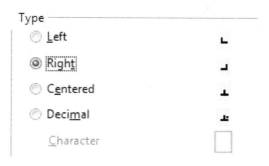

Figure 6

Step 6: Along the left side of the menu, Impress allows the user to type in the desired position of where the tab will be placed on the Ruler. Once the preferred position has been identified, click **New** and then click **OK**. The new tab will be placed onto the Ruler.

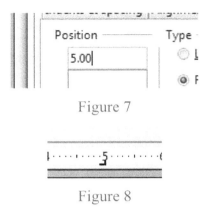

Figure 7

Figure 8

Growth & Assessment

1. What does the Ruler option do?

2. What are the four different types of tabs available in Impress?

3. The Ruler option is an easy way to set and adjust tabs in a slide.

   a. TRUE

   b. FALSE

Section 1.7 – Using Tips and the Help Dialog Box

Section Objectives:

- Learn about getting help with Impress using tips.

- Learn about getting help with Impress using the Help dialog box.

Using Tips

OpenOffice Impress has features that help the user identify tools and perform certain tasks. **Tips** is a feature that displays the name of a tool when the cursor is positioned over its icon. Tips not only contain the names of buttons, but the feature also provides other useful information. For example, while scrolling through a presentation, Tips displays the current slide number.

Figure 1

What's This? is a tool in Impress that will display extended tips about the buttons available on the application's toolbars. What's This? is also helpful when trying to understand the functionality of a command or the different uses of a button.

The **What's This?** feature can be accessed by opening the Help menu and selecting **What's This?**. Once the feature is selected, position the cursor over any button to display the button's description. For example, if the What's This? feature is selected, and the cursor is positioned over the Spell Check button (located on the formatting toolbar), the extended tips for the Spell Check feature will be displayed.

If a user would like to enable extended tips so that they are always displayed, this can be done by opening the Tools drop-down menu, selecting Options, choosing General (on the left, under OpenOffice.org), and enabling the "tips" and "extended tips" checkboxes. By enabling these features, users are able to identify the name of a button and its functionality without opening the Help menus.

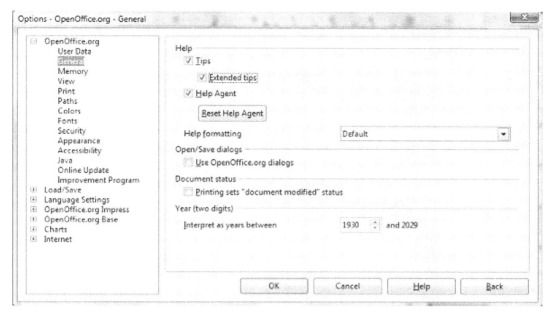

Figure 2

Using the Help Dialog Box

In situations where the What's This? feature is enabled but more information is needed, the information can be found in the **Help** dialog box. Accessing the Help dialog Box is done by clicking the **Help** button (the small question mark), located in the top right-hand corner of the **Toolbar**.

Figure 3

For example, if a user needs help saving a presentation, the first thing the user would do is click the **Help** button. Once the Help button has been clicked, the user would follow the steps below to obtain the needed information. For the purpose of this example, follow the steps below to gain a better understanding of this process.

Step 1: Click the **Find** tab, located along the top of the Help dialog box.

Step 2: In the **Search** textbox, type "**Saving a Document**."

OpenOffice.org Impress		▼

Contents	Index	**Find**	Bookmarks

Search term

Saving A Document	▼	Find

☐ Complete words only

☐ Find in headings only

Figure 4

Step 3: Press **Enter** or click **Find**. The search results will appear in the **Help** dialog box.

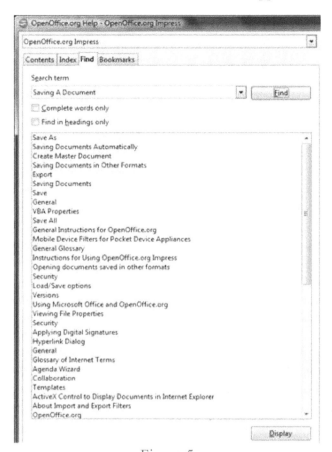

Figure 5

Step 4: From the list of topics on the screen, select **Save As**. A description of how to perform a 'Save As' will be displayed on the screen.

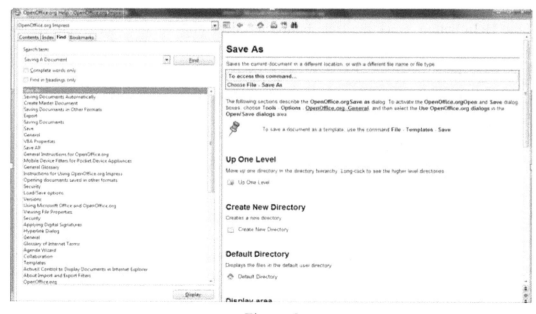

Figure 6

Step 5: When the needed information has been obtained, close the Help dialog box.

> **Note** – The same information can be found in the **Contents** and **Index** tabs which are located in the Help dialog box.

Growth & Assessment

1. What button would a user click to get help with something?

2. The What's This? feature can be accessed by opening the Help menu and selecting What's This?.

   a. TRUE

   b. FALSE

3. What does the Help button look like?

Section 1.8 – Creating a Blank Presentation

Section Objective:

- Learn how to create a blank presentation.

Create a Blank Presentation

When OpenOffice Impress is opened, the application displays a blank Title slide as the first slide in the presentation. This is convenient because it allows the user to start creating a new presentation as soon as the application opens. If the application is already open, a user can still easily create a presentation. The following steps outline how a user can create a presentation from both starting points.

Steps for Creating a Presentation when Impress Opens:

Step 1: Open Impress from the **Start** menu. As stated above, a blank Title slide will appear as the first slide in the presentation.

Step 2: Click the arrow next to **Layout** on the **Tasks** pane found along the right side of the application window. This will expand the **Layout** pane.

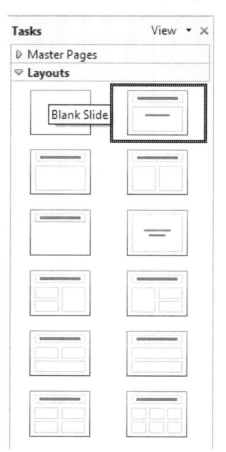

Figure 1

Step 3: From the Layout pane, select the preferred layout for the first slide of the presentation. Once it is selected, the new layout will replace the Title slide in the presentation.

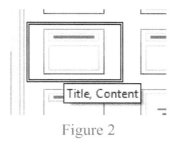

Figure 2

Steps for Creating a New Presentation from an Existing Presentation:

As stated above, Impress allows users to create a new presentation once the application has already been opened. The following steps outline how this is done by incorporating one of OpenOffice Impress's many themes.

Step 1: Click **File**, located on the Menu Bar.

Step 2: From the File drop-down menu, select **New** and then select **Templates and Documents**. The **Templates and Documents** dialog box will appear.

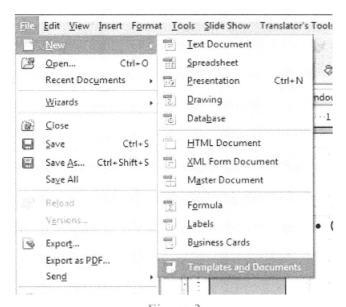

Figure 3

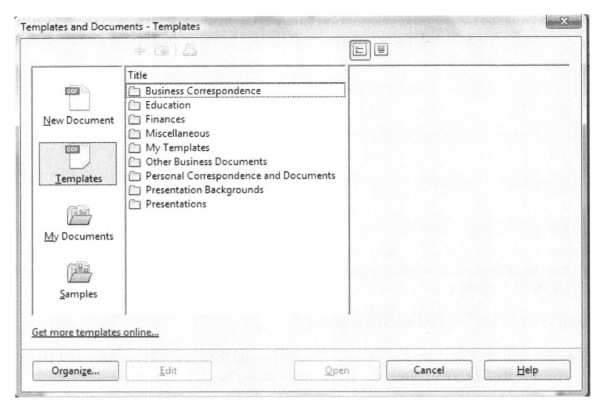

Figure 4

Step 3: From the column of options along the left-hand side of the dialog box, click **Templates**.

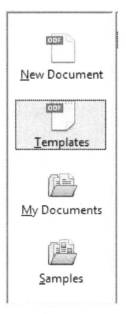

Figure 5

Step 4: In the **Title** pane, which is the middle window, select **Presentation Backgrounds**.

Figure 6

Step 5: From the options provided, select the desired background. The selected background will be applied to the new blank presentation.

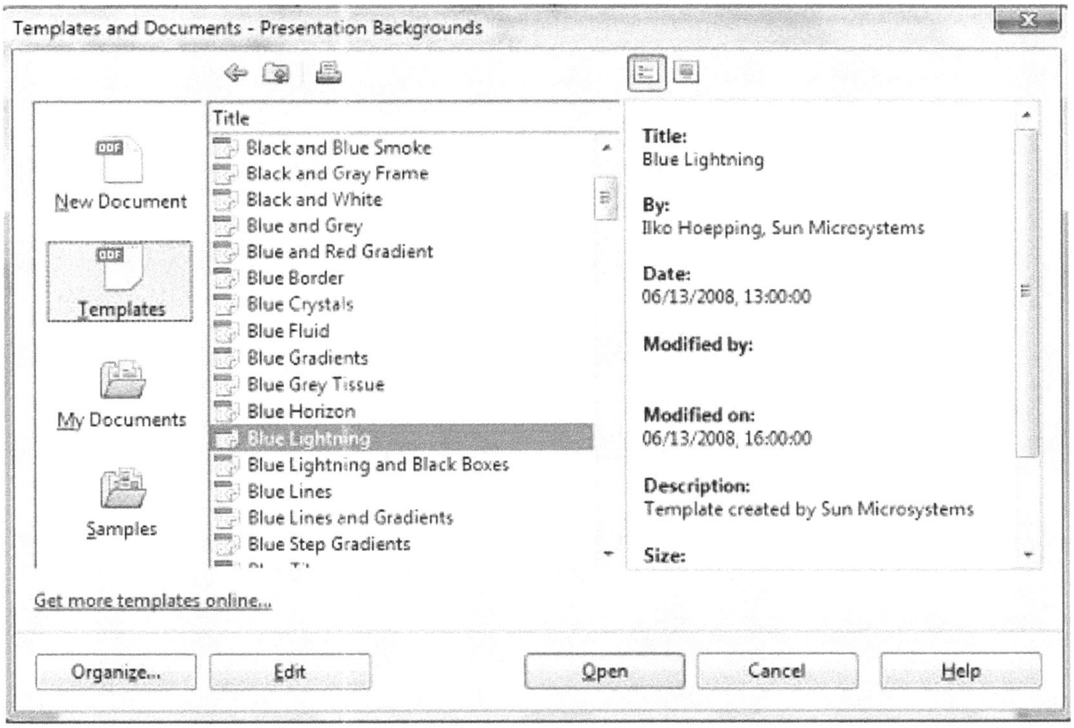

Figure 7

Step 6: Once a background has been selected, click the **Open** button. A new blank presentation will be created with the selected background as the theme.

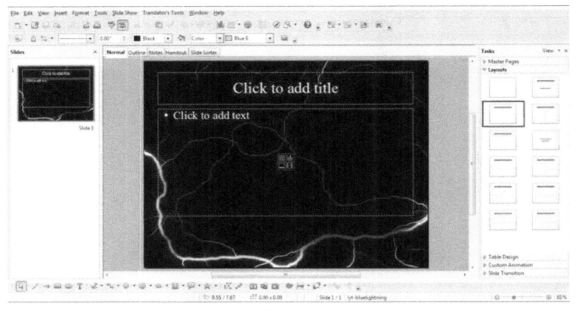

Figure 8

Growth & Assessment

1. Users are able to create a presentation when Impress is open.

   a. TRUE

   b. FALSE

2. What is the first slide of a new Impress presentation?

3. Why is it convenient to have a blank Title slide?

Section 1.9 – Creating a Presentation Using a Template

Section Objective:

- Learn how to create a presentation using a template.

Using a Template

OpenOffice Impress provides **Templates**, which are presentations with a pre-designed slide format. These templates can be used as a starting point for a variety of Impress presentations, such as business proposals, technical specs, and product descriptions. OpenOffice Impress features a variety of free templates that users can download. The following steps guide users through downloading a packet of templates which can be used for future presentations in Impress.

Step 1: Go to the following link: *http://extensions.services.openoffice.org/node/1338*. This link will navigate the user to the OpenOffice **Template Pack** download page.

Figure 1

Step 2: Click the **Get It!** button to be directed to the **Download** page.

Figure 2

Step 3: Click the manual download link to begin the downloading process.

Figure 3

Step 4: When prompted, click the **Open** button on the **File Download** window.

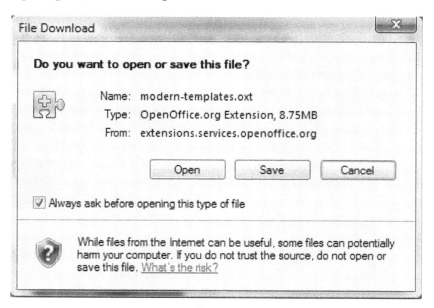

Figure 4

Step 5: The next prompt will ask the user to verify the installation of the **Modern Impress Templates**. Click **OK** and then click **Accept** to accept the license agreement.

Figure 5

32

Step 6: The final window, the **Extension Manager**, will show that the Template Pack was added to Impress. Click **Close**, and begin using the new templates.

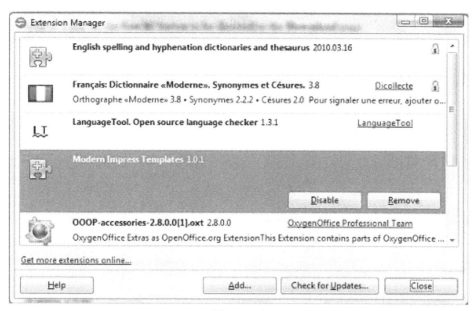

Figure 6

Using Templates to Create a New Presentation

The following steps will outline how a user can create a new presentation using the templates downloaded above.

Step 1: Click **File**, located on the Menu Bar.

Step 2: From the File drop-down menu, scroll over **New** and select **Templates and Documents**. The **Templates and Documents** dialog box will appear.

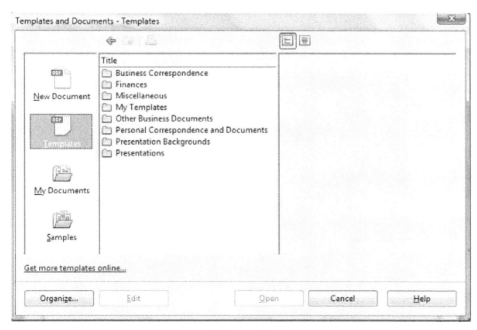

Figure 7

Step 3: On the left side of the dialog box, click **Templates** and then choose **Presentations** from the available choices.

Step 4: The templates within the **Presentations** folder will be displayed in the window. Select the preferred template.

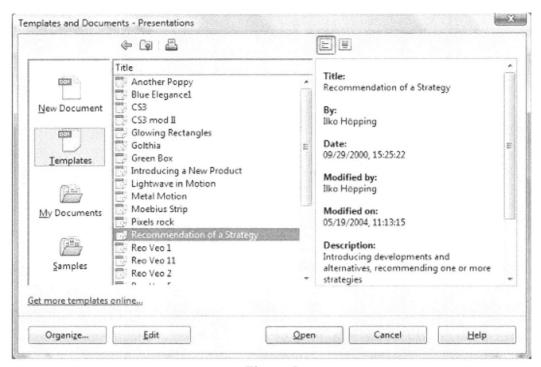

Figure 8

Step 5: Click **Open**. The template will be applied to the new presentation.

Note – Multiple slides are made for the user once a new presentation is created.

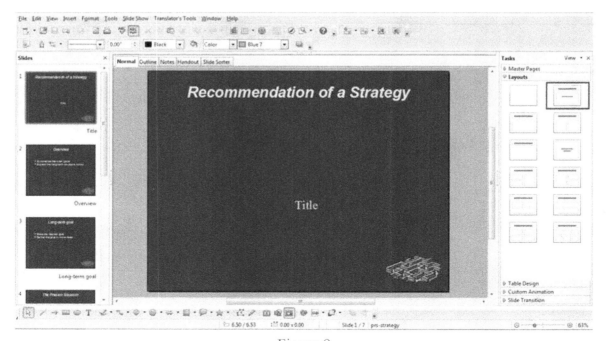

Figure 9

Growth & Assessment

1. When a new presentation is created, only one slide is made for the user.

    a. TRUE

    b. FALSE

2. What is a template?

3. How are templates used?

4. Give an example of a presentation template.

Section 1.10 – Adding Textboxes to a Slide

Section Objective:

- Learn how to add and use textboxes in a slide.

Adding Textboxes to a Slide

When text needs to be added to a slide in OpenOffice Impress, a textbox needs to be inserted. Textboxes appear in many different forms, and depending on the slide layout, some textboxes are already inserted into the slide. If this is the case, the user can enter text into the textbox and start creating the presentation.

If a user is in a situation where a textbox is needed, Impress allows the user to create their own textbox and customize its dimensions. The following steps outline how this is done in OpenOffice Impress.

Step 1: Open Impress and create a new blank presentation. Change the first slide from the default layout to a completely blank layout, without any textboxes.

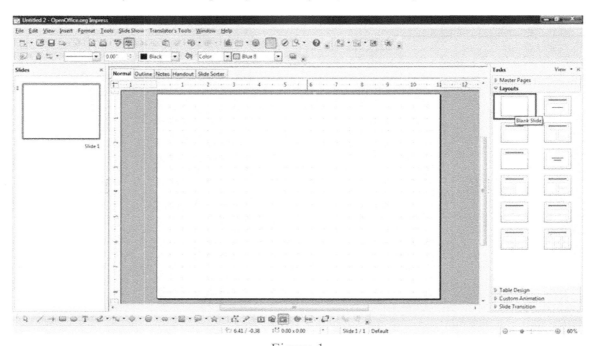

Figure 1

Step 2: Click on the **T** found in the **Drawing** toolbar at the bottom of the application window. The cursor will change to an insertion point.

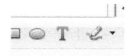

Figure 2

Step 3: Within the slide, click and drag the cursor to create the dimensions of the needed textbox.

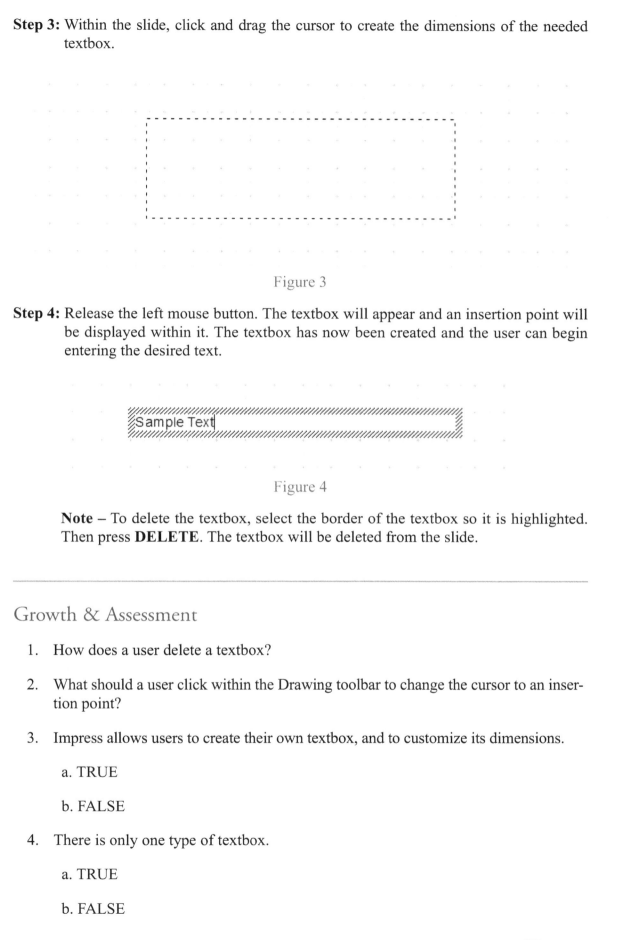

Figure 3

Step 4: Release the left mouse button. The textbox will appear and an insertion point will be displayed within it. The textbox has now been created and the user can begin entering the desired text.

Figure 4

Note – To delete the textbox, select the border of the textbox so it is highlighted. Then press **DELETE**. The textbox will be deleted from the slide.

Growth & Assessment

1. How does a user delete a textbox?

2. What should a user click within the Drawing toolbar to change the cursor to an insertion point?

3. Impress allows users to create their own textbox, and to customize its dimensions.

    a. TRUE

    b. FALSE

4. There is only one type of textbox.

    a. TRUE

    b. FALSE

Section 1.11 – Adding Slides to a Presentation

Section Objective:

- Learn how to add slides to a presentation.

Adding Slides to a Presentation

Most presentations created in OpenOffice Impress will have more than one slide. If a user is creating a presentation with multiple slides, and a template is not being used, the additional slides need to be manually added to the presentation. This section outlines the necessary steps for adding slides to a presentation through the **Slides** tab and the Menu Bar.

Steps for Adding Slides through the Slides Tab:

Note – By default, the new slide's layout and theme will be the same as the preceding slide.

Step 1: In the **Slides** tab, located on the left-hand side of the application window, right-click the slide after which the new slide will be inserted, and then select **New Slide**. A new slide will be inserted into the presentation.

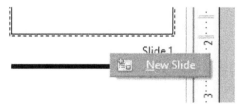

Figure 1

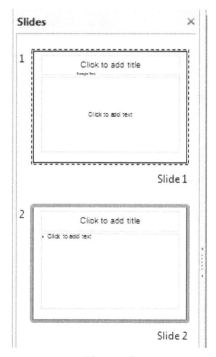

Figure 2

Step 2: To modify the slide layout, click the **Layouts** tab found in the **Tasks** pane. Here, select the preferred slide type that will be inserted into the presentation.

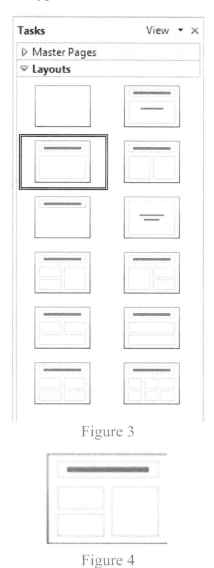

Figure 3

Figure 4

Steps for Adding Slides through the Menu Bar:

Step 1: Click **Insert**, located on the Menu Bar.

Step 2: From in the Insert drop-down menu, click **Slide**. A new slide will be inserted into the presentation.

Figure 5

Note – Like before, the new slide entered into the presentation will be the same style as the previous slide. The slide's layout can be modified by accessing the **Layouts** tab.

Growth & Assessment

1. If a new slide is inserted, it will not have the same style as the previous slide.

    a. TRUE

    b. FALSE

2. What should a user click to modify the slide layout?

3. Most presentations created in OpenOffice Impress will have one slide.

    a. TRUE

    b. FALSE

Section 1.12 – Saving a Presentation

Section Objectives:

- Learn how to save a presentation.

- Learn how to save a presentation in different formats.

Saving a Presentation

In OpenOffice Impress, the **Save** and **Save As** commands are located within the **File** menu on the Menu Bar. If a user is saving the presentation for the first time, both selections will take the user to the **Save As** dialog box. This section will outline the necessary steps for saving a presentation and will also explain how a user can save the presentation in different formats.

Steps for Saving a Presentation in Impress:

Step 1: Create a new Impress presentation and type the desired text into the Title slide.

Step 2: Click **File**, located on the Menu Bar.

Step 3: From the File drop-down menu, select **Save As**. The **Save As** dialog box will appear.

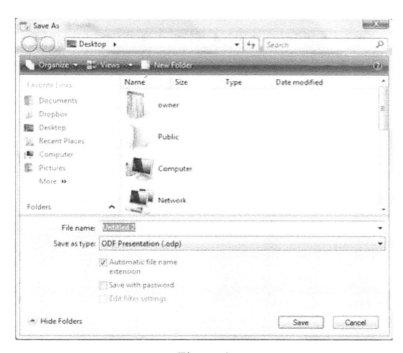

Figure 1

Step 4: From the **Save In** pull-down list, located in the dialog box, choose the preferred folder in which the presentation will be saved.

Step 5: In the **File Name** textbox, enter the preferred name and then click **Save**. Once the presentation has been saved, the file name will be visible in application's title bar.

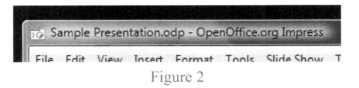

Figure 2

Note – Once a presentation has been saved, the user can use the keyboard shortcut **CTRL + S** to save the presentation while working on it to ensure that forward progress is not lost.

Steps for Saving a Presentation in a Different File Format:

In OpenOffice Impress, by default, presentations are saved with an **.odp** file extension, which stands for Open Document Format (ODF) Presentation. Impress also allows users to save the presentation in different file formats which is useful when working with other applications such as Microsoft's PowerPoint. The following steps outline how a user can save a presentation in a different file format.

Step 1: Using the same presentation as above, access the **File** drop-down menu, which is located on the Menu Bar.

Step 2: From the File drop-down menu, select **Save As**. The **Save As** dialog box will appear.

Step 3: From the **Save In** pull-down list, select the preferred folder in which the presentation will be saved.

Step 4: In the **File Name** textbox, enter the preferred name.

Step 5: In the **Save As** type pull-down list, select the preferred file format from the available options. Once the preferred file type has been selected, click **Save**. The presentation will be saved in the selected format.

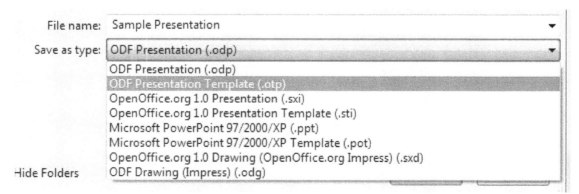

Figure 3

Growth & Assessment

1. What is the keyboard shortcut used to access the Save As dialog box?

2. What is the file extension for default Impress presentations?

3. In OpenOffice Impress, the Save and Save As commands are located within the File drop-down menu on the Menu Bar.

   a. TRUE

   b. FALSE

Section 1.13 – Creating a Slide Master

Section Objective:

- Learn how to create and customize a Slide Master.

The Slide Master

When creating a presentation in OpenOffice Impress, one important aspect of the presentation is consistency. Consistency adds credibility, as well as organization to a presentation. A consistent look can be achieved quickly by customizing the Slide Master, rather than customizing each slide individually. When the Slide Master is set up before creating the entire presentation, every additional slide added to the presentation will be based on the Slide Master created in the beginning, which will ensure consistency.

To customize a Slide Master, the user must specify the placement of text and objects that will be placed into the subsequent slides. This section will explain the steps for creating the Slide Master, as well as techniques that can be used to modify the Slide Master.

Steps for Creating the Slide Master:

Step 1: Open Impress and create a new presentation.

Step 2: Click **View**, located on the Menu Bar.

Step 3: From the View drop-down menu, scroll the cursor over **Master**, and then select **Slide Master**.

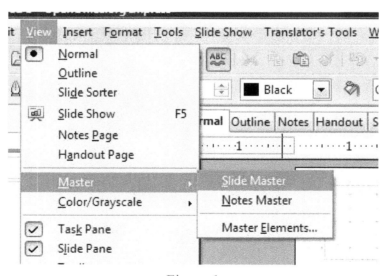

Figure 1

Step 4: When the Slide Master view opens, a blank **Slide Master** will appear on the application window. To modify the blank Slide Master, refer to the steps below.

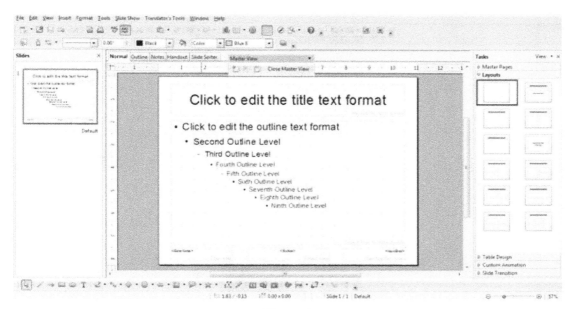

Figure 2

Steps for Modifying the Slide Master:

As stated above, OpenOffice Impress allows users to make modifications to the Slide Master once it has been created. The following steps outline some of the possible modifications users can perform on the Slide Master.

Step 1: If the user wants to make modifications to the **Font**, **Size**, and/or **Color** of the text in the slides, click anywhere within the Slide Master and select **Format**, and then click **Character**. The **Character** dialog box will appear and the user has the ability to modify the Master Slide's text.

Figure 3

Step 2: Select the **Master Pages** tab along the right-hand side of the application window. From the **Available for Use** portion of the tab, select the preferred theme for the Slide Master.

Figure 4

Step 3: Set the page orientation for the Master Slide by accessing the **Format** menu and selecting **Page…**. From the **Page Setup** dialog box, the user has the ability to change the orientation of the slides in the presentation.

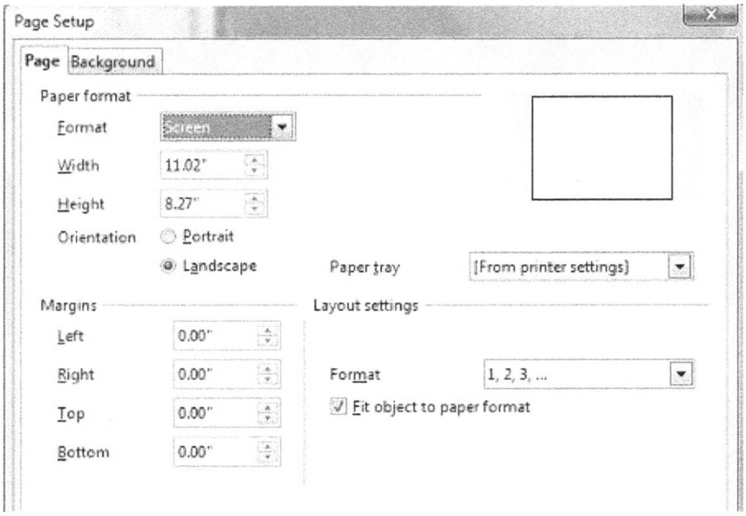

Figure 5

Once all of the desired modifications have been made to the Slide Master, click **Close Master View** to return to the presentation.

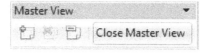

Figure 6

Growth & Assessment

1. What does consistency do for a slide?

2. How can a consistent look be quickly achieved?

3. When the Slide Master is set up before creating the entire presentation, every additional slide added to the presentation will be based on the Slide Master.

    a. TRUE

    b. FALSE

Section 1.14 – Changing the Slide Layout and Presentation Theme

Section Objectives:

- Learn how to change the slide layout.

- Learn how to change the presentation theme.

Changing the Slide Layout and Presentation Theme

Making modifications to a presentation in OpenOffice Impress can be done quickly and easily. One of the most common modifications is changing the slide Layout and presentation Theme. A Theme is a particular style that uses colors, textures, and font styles. This section will explain how a user can modify both of these features while working on an Impress presentation.

Steps for Changing the Slide Layout:

Before following the steps below, create a new presentation in Impress using the **Introducing a new Product** template.

Step 1: From the **Slides** pane along the left-hand side of the application window, select the preferred slide which the new layout will be applied to. For this example, select the first slide in the presentation.

Step 2: In the **Tasks** pane along the right-hand side of the application window, click **Layouts** to expand the **Layouts** pane.

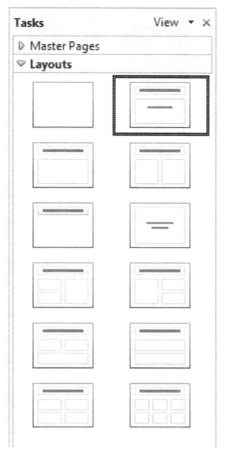

Figure 1

Step 3: From the **Layouts** pane, click on the desired layout which will be applied to the selected slide. For this example choose the **Title and 2 Content** layout. Once the layout has been clicked, it will be applied to the selected slide.

Figure 2

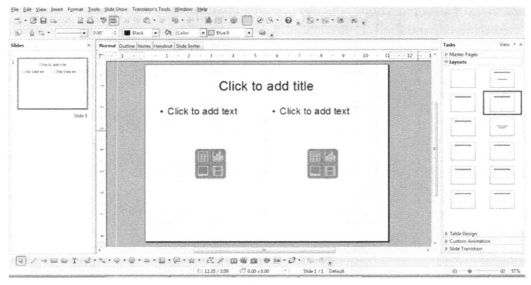

Figure 3

Steps for Changing the Presentation Theme:

Note – Unlike applying a new slide layout, the steps below will not change a single slide, but instead, change the theme of the entire presentation.

Step 1: Select any slide in the presentation.

Step 2: In the **Tasks** pane along the right side of the application window, click **Master Pages** to expand the **Master Pages** pane.

Figure 4

Step 3: From the **Master Pages** pane, click the preferred theme which will apply to the entire presentation. For this example choose the **Blue Crystals** theme. Once the theme has been selected, it will be applied to the entire presentation.

Figure 5

Growth & Assessment

1. Making modifications to a presentation in OpenOffice Impress can be done quickly and easily.

    a. TRUE

    b. FALSE

2. Once the theme has been clicked, it will be applied to only one slide.

    a. TRUE

    b. FALSE

3. What is a theme?

Section 1.15 – Finding and Replacing Text

Section Objective:

- Learn how to find and replace text in a slide.

Finding and Replacing Text in a Slide

In OpenOffice Impress, finding specific text in the slides can be difficult when working with a large presentation. Impress solves this problem with the **Find** tool. Impress allows users to find specific text in a presentation a variety of ways, which is helpful when trying to located needed information.

Another tool that is helpful, especially when editing large presentations, is the **Replace** tool. The Replace tool works with the Find tool to locate the desired text and replace it with different text. This section will allow the user to practice finding and replacing text hidden within the slides of a presentation. Follow the steps below to learn how to use the Find and Replace tool.

Note – In order to follow the steps below, open an Impress presentation and type "house" into the title slide.

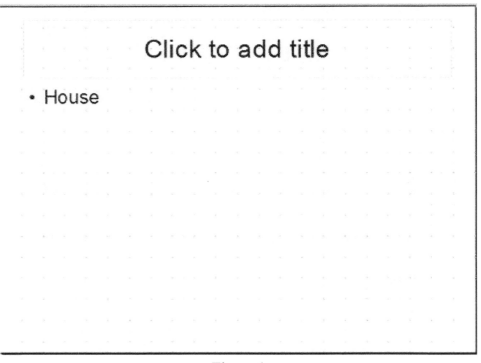

Figure 1

Steps for Using the Find Tool:

Step 1: Click **Edit**, located on the Menu Bar.

Step 2: From the Edit drop-down menu, select **Find & Replace**. The **Find & Replace** dialog box will appear.

> **Note** – The keyboard shortcut **CTRL + F** will also open the **Find & Replace** dialog box.

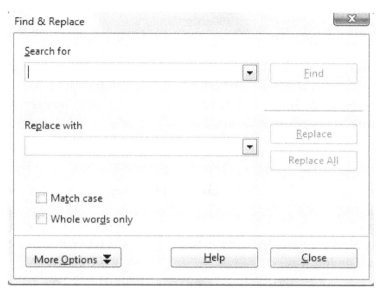

Figure 2

Step 3: In the **Search For** textbox, type "**house**."

Step 4: Click **Find**. The first occurrence of "**house**" will be highlighted in the presentation.

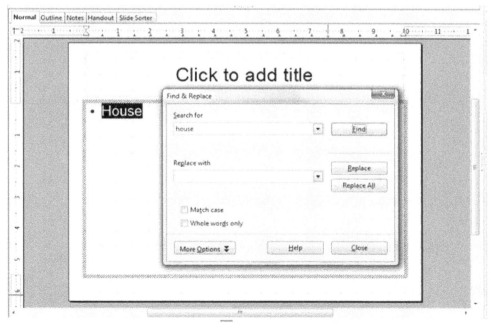

Figure 3

Step 5: To find more occurrences of the word, repeat **Step 4**. Every time **Find** is clicked, the **Find & Replace** tool will highlight the next occurrence of the word in the presentation.

Step 6: Once all of the occurrences of "**house**" have been found, click **Close**.

> **Note -** When Impress has shown every occurrence of the searched for text, a dialog box will appear with the message "OpenOffice Impress has searched to the end of the presentation. Do you want to continue at the beginning?"

Steps for using the Replace Tool:

With the **Find & Replace** tool, Impress allows users to replace all occurrences of a particular word or phrase, or look at each occurrence before deciding which to replace. In the steps below, search for the word "**house**;" however, this time replace "**house**" with "**home**." Follow the steps below to complete this process.

Step 1: Select **Edit** on the Menu Bar.

Step 2: Within the Edit drop-down menu, click **Find & Replace**. The **Find & Replace** dialog box will appear.

> **Note –** As stated above, the keyboard shortcut **CTRL + F** will also open the **Find & Replace** dialog box.

Step 3: In the **Search for** textbox, enter "**house**."

Step 4: In the **Replace with** textbox, enter "**home**."

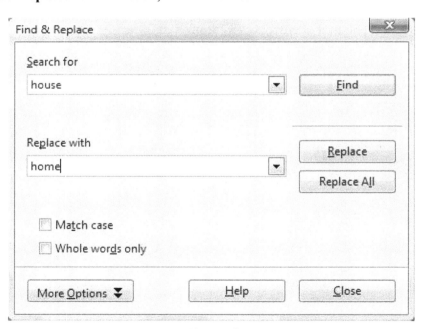

Figure 4

Step 5: To find the first occurrence of "**house**," click **Find**. The first occurrence will be highlighted, as it was before.

Step 6: To replace the text, click **Replace**. To leave the text as it is and proceed to the next occurrence, click **Find**.

Step 7: Repeat **Step 4** until all desired replacements have been made and then click **Close**.

> **Note** – To replace all of the occurrences of the searched for word, click **Replace All** in the **Find & Replace** dialog box. Once this has been clicked, all occurrences of the searched for word will be replaced.

Growth & Assessment

1. What does the Find tool do?

2. The keyboard shortcut to access the Find tool is CTRL + F.

   a. TRUE

   b. FALSE

3. The Replace feature allows users to replace occurrences of one text with another.

   a. TRUE

   b. FALSE

4. What does the Replace All feature do?

Unit Two

Section 2.1 – Checking Spelling

Section Objective:

- Learn how to check the spelling of slides in a presentation.

Check Spelling in a Presentation

In OpenOffice Impress, when a word is spelled incorrectly, the Impress dictionary automatically underlines the word with a wavy red line. This is helpful when editing slides because this feature draws the user's eye to the error. There are a couple ways to correct misspelled words in Impress. One way is by using the Quick Menu, and the other way is by accessing the Spelling dialog box. Both of these options are described in the steps below.

Wronng speling

Figure 1

Correct Misspelled Words by Using the Quick Menu

Correcting misspelled words by using the Quick Menu allows users to modify misspelled words quickly while working on the presentation. To use the Quick Menu, **Right-click** the word and select the appropriate command from the options listed below:

- **Spelling Suggestions** – Gives suggestions for correcting the misspelled word.

- **Spelling...** – Opens the Spelling dialog box.

- **Ignore All** – Ignores that instance of the misspelled word and every other instance found in the presentation.

- **Add** – Adds the word to a dictionary of the user's choice.

- **AutoCorrect** – Provides word choices for the AutoCorrect function.

Figure 2

Correct Misspelled Words by Using the Spelling Dialog Box

As stated above, Impress provides a second option for correcting misspelled words; the Spelling dialog box. The Spelling dialog box is helpful when editing a presentation after it has been created. The dialog box will remain open as the user moves through the presentation and makes the necessary corrections. The following steps outline how a user can use this tool to correct the spelling within a presentation.

Step 1: Click **Tools**, located on the Menu Bar.

Step 2: From the Tools drop-down menu, select **Spelling…**. The Spelling dialog box will appear.

Figure 3

Step 3: Choose the desired selection for each misspelling and then select the action that will take place. Some of the available options are listed below.

> **Note** – The Spelling dialog box includes all Quick Menu options as well as the following:

- **Ignore Once** – Ignores that particular occurrence of that word.

- **Change** – Changes the word to the selected suggestion.

- **Change All** – Changes all identical misspellings to the selected suggestion.

Figure 4

Growth & Assessment

1. What is one way to correct a misspelled words?

2. When the Impress dictionary recognizes a word as misspelled, the word is automatically underlined with a wavy red line.

    a. TRUE

    b. FALSE

3. How is the Spelling dialog box opened?

4. What other options does the Spelling dialog box provide?

Section 2.2 – Creating Handouts

Section Objective:

- Learn how to create slide handouts.

Creating Slide Handouts

OpenOffice Impress allows users to print out slide handouts for their presentation. Printing out and distributing handouts during an Impress presentation is a great way to help the audience follow along and take notes. Handouts can be formatted similar to the Slide or Title masters, allowing the customization of fonts, background, and the layout. Formatting a Handout Master can be useful if a user wants to include a logo, emblem or slide number on the handouts. The following steps outline how to create handouts, modify the layout and text for a presentation.

Creating Handouts and Modifying the Layout

Step 1: Create a new Impress presentation.

Step 2: Click **View**, located on the Menu Bar.

Step 3: From the View drop-down menu, click **Handout Page**. The window will change to **Handout** view and the **Handout Layouts** pane will be displayed along the right-hand side of the window.

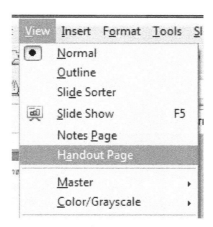

Figure 1

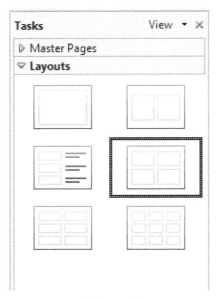

Figure 2

Step 4: From Handout Layouts pane, click through and view the different layout options available. Once a layout is clicked, the layout of the handout will automatically change.

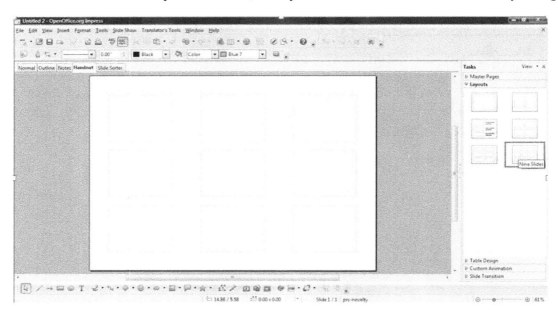

Figure 3

Modifying the Text and Adding Headers and Footers

OpenOffice Impress, as with regular text, allows users to modify the **Font**, **Size**, and **Color** of the text on the handouts. Impress also allows users to add a **Header** and/or **Footer** to the handouts. Handouts with a Header and/or Footer may be more useful for giving the audience certain information, such as the date and time, slide number, or the title of the presentation. Header and Footer zones automatically appear on every handout page. If a user would like to add information to these two areas, they can double-click in the Header/ Footer zone and type the desired information. The information entered into the Header and/ or Footer will appear on every slide.

Figure 4

Growth & Assessment

1. Why is formatting a Handout Master useful?

2. Users are not able to modify the font, size, and color of the text on a handouts.

   a. TRUE

   b. FALSE

3. Within which drop-down menu is the Handout Page feature located?

4. Handouts can be formatted similar to the Slide or Title masters, allowing the customization of fonts, background, and placeholders.

   a. TRUE

   b. FALSE

Section 2.3 – Printing in Impress

Section Objectives:

- Learn how to prepare slides for print.

- Learn how to print an Impress presentation.

Prepare and Print Slides in Impress

OpenOffice Impress offers many different printing options for presentations. Depending on the user's presentation, it may be helpful to print out some or all of the slides. Printing out the slides is helpful when presenting because it allows for the audience to follow along and create notes. Doing this not only engages the audience, but also allows them to get more out of the presentation.

Before printing slides, users must set up how the slides will be printed. Users can identify the output medium, as well as the orientation of the slides, notes, handouts, and outlines. Once this is done, the slides can be printed for the presentation. This section will outline how to prepare slides and print them in OpenOffice Impress.

Preparing Slides for Printing

Step 1: Create a new Impress presentation with multiple slides.

Step 2: Click **File**, located on the Menu Bar.

Step 3: From in the File drop-down menu, select **Print…**. The **Print** dialog box will open with the **General** tab selected.

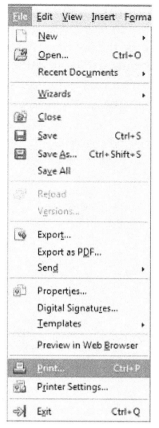

Figure 1

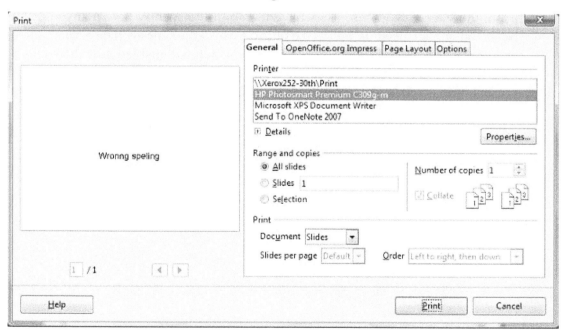

Figure 2

Step 4: Click on the **OpenOffice Impress** tab at the top of the Print dialog box. From this tab users have the ability to select special fields which will be included on the printout. Special fields include the file name, date, and any hidden pages. Users can also select whether the printouts will be in color, black and white, or grayscale. The final option in this tab is to determine the size of the slides on each printed page. Once the desired options have been selected, click on the **Page Layout** tab.

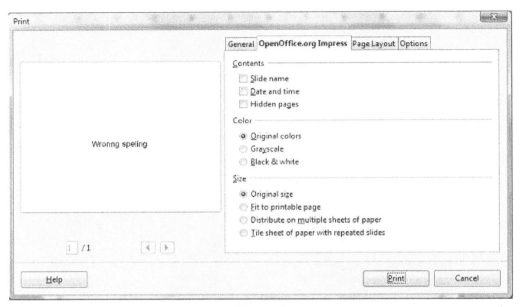

Figure 3

Step 5: From the Page Layout tab, users have the ability to specify how many slides will be shown on each page, as well as the order in which the slides will be printed. Impress provides a preview section in the dialog box which will display how the slides will be laid out on the page. Once all of the preferred options have been selected, the presentation is ready to be printed. Follow the steps below to learn how to print the presentation.

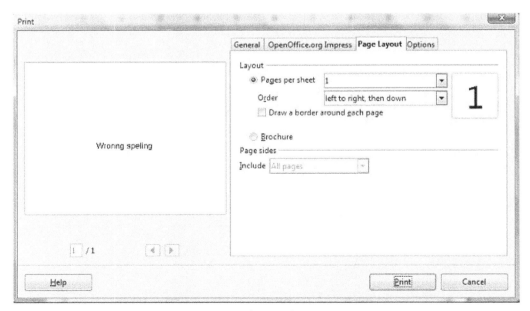

Figure 4

Step 1: Click the **General** tab, located in the Print dialog box.

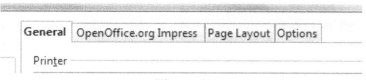

Figure 5

Step 2: In the **Number of Copies** selection area, located on the right side of the **Range and Copies** portion of the dialog box, enter the preferred number of copies. Do this by using the nudge buttons or by manually entering the desired number of copies.

Note – The default number of copies is one.

Figure 6

Step 3: On the left side of the **Range and Copies** portion of the dialog box, select which slides will be printed. The user has the ability to print all of the slides in the presentation, a specific range of slides, or the current slide selected.

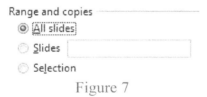

Figure 7

Note – If a user chooses to print specific slides, they must separate a sequential list of slides with a hyphen (1-3) and a non-sequential range using commas (1,5,8). The figure below displays the entered text that would print slides 1 through 5, as well as slides 7, 9, and 11.

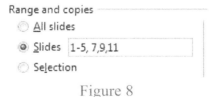

Figure 8

Step 4: From the **Document** pull-down list, the user can select what will actually be printed. **Slides**, the default selection, will print out all of the slides in the presentation. The other options available will also print the presentation, but may also include additional information such as handouts and notes. After selecting the preferred option from the Document pull-down list, click **Print** to print the presentation.

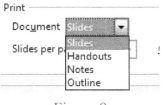

Figure 9

Growth & Assessment

1. What does the OpenOffice Impress tab allow users to do?

2. The Page Layout tab allows users to specify how many slides will be displayed on each page, as well as the order in which they would like them to print.

   a. TRUE

   b. FALSE

3. When identifying which slides need to be printed, what character is entered to separate a non-sequential range of slides?

4. When selecting specific slides to be printed, how would the following slides be represented within the Range and copies portion of the Print dialog box?

   2,3,4,6,12,14,15,16,20,21,25

Section 2.4 – Using the Fontwork Gallery and ClipArt

Section Objectives:

- Learn how to use the Fontwork Gallery.

- Learn how to insert ClipArt into a slide.

The Fontwork Gallery

The Fontwork Gallery allows users to create graphic text art objects which can be inserted into Impress presentations. This is a helpful feature when a user is trying to express creativity or draw attention to something within the presentation. The Fontwork Gallery offers many options for text art objects, such as positioning, size, area, and other various settings that allow a user to create a unique graphic object for a presentation. The following steps outline how a user can incorporate Fontwork into a presentation.

Step 1: Click on the **Fontwork Gallery** icon from the **Drawing Toolbar**. The **Fontwork Gallery** dialog box will appear.

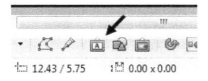

Figure 1

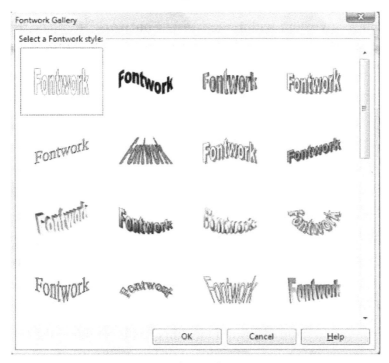

Figure 2

Note – If the Drawing Toolbar isn't visible on the screen, go to **View > Toolbars > Drawing** to make it visible.

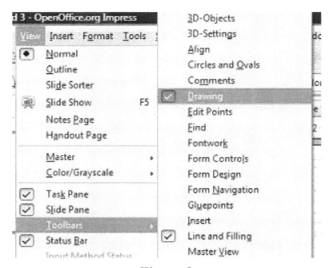

Figure 3

Step 2: Select the preferred design to insert into the presentation, and then click **OK**. The word "**Fontwork**" will be inserted into the current slide.

Figure 4

Step 3: Double-click anywhere within the word "**Fontwork**" to place the insertion point. Once the insertion point has been placed within the word, the user can replace "**Fontwork**" with the needed text.

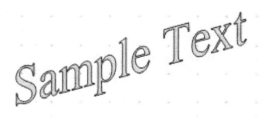

Figure 5

Step 4: Resize the inserted Fontwork object. This is done by dragging the eight blue squares, referred to as *handles*, to adjust the size of the graphic object.

Step 5: Distort the inserted Fontwork object. Along with the eight blue squares, there will be a yellow dot on the object. Position the cursor over the yellow dot and the cursor will change into a hand symbol. Once this has been done, the user can distort the Fontwork object by dragging the dot in different directions.

Step 6: Once the Fontwork object has been resized and distorted, the object can be moved within the slide. This can be done by positioning the cursor over the object until the cursor transforms into the dragging symbol. Once this has happened, the newly created Fontwork object can be placed in the desired location within the slide.

Inserting ClipArt

OpenOffice Impress not only allows users to incorporate graphic text art from the Fontwork gallery, but also allows users to insert free ClipArt into a presentation. By adding a free extension to the application, users can access a collection of different ClipArt which can be used in Impress. The following steps outline how to download the free extension and add a variety of ClipArt to the application.

Step 1: Access the OpenOffice ClipArt extension page which can be found at the following link: *http://extensions.services.openoffice.org/en/project/oxygenoffice-gallery*

Figure 6

Step 2: Click **Get It!** to be directed to the **Download** page.

Figure 7

Step 3: Click on the manual download link to begin the download.

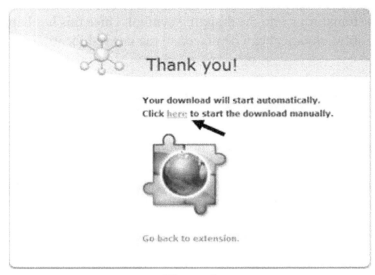

Figure 8

Step 4: When prompted, click **Open** on the File Download window.

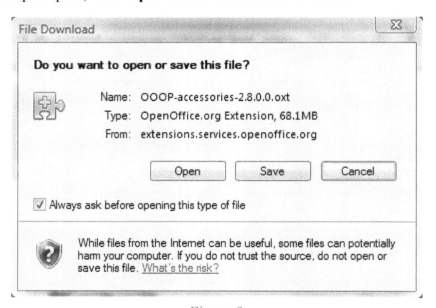

Figure 9

Step 5: Click **OK** and then click **Accept** to accept the license agreement and begin installing **OOOP-Accessories**.

Figure 10

Step 6: The Extension Manager window will show that **OOOP-Accessories** has been added to Impress. Click **Close** and begin using the new graphics.

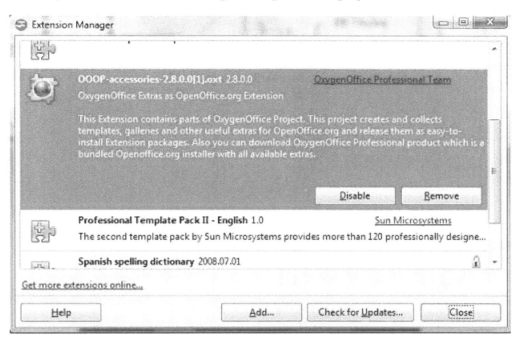

Figure 11

Once ClipArt has been added to Impress, new ClipArt can be added to the presentation by browsing through the **Gallery**. The following steps explain how this is done.

Step 1: Create a new Impress presentation and click **Tools**, which is located on the Menu Bar.

Step 2: From the **Tools** drop-down menu, click **Gallery**. This will cause the ClipArt task pane to appear at the top of the page window.

Figure 12

Step 3: Along the left-hand side of the task pane, there will be folders displaying the different types of ClipArt available. Click on the desired type of ClipArt.

Figure 13

Step 4: Scroll through the selected ClipArt folder and view the different images that are available. Once an image has been selected, click on it with the left mouse button and drag the image into the slide.

Growth & Assessment

1. Graphics and colorful word art cannot be integrated into Impress slides.

    a. TRUE

    b. FALSE

2. What is the Fontwork Gallery used for?

3. How do users make the Drawing Toolbar visible on the screen?

4. How do users make the ClipArt task pane appear at the top of the page window?

Section 2.5 – Adding GIFs and Sounds

Section Objectives:

- Learn how to add animated GIFs.

- Learn how to add Sounds.

Adding GIFs

In OpenOffice Impress, it is possible to add movies or animated GIF (Graphical Interchange Format) images to a presentation. Adding GIFs to a presentation allow users to create more complex and eye catching slides without having to do too much extra work. The following steps explain how to add a GIF to an Impress presentation.

Before following the steps below, create a new Impress presentation and change the layout to a blank slide.

Step 1: Click **Insert**, located on the Menu Bar.

Step 2: From the Insert drop-down menu, scroll the cursor over **Picture** and select **From File...**. The **Insert Picture** dialog box will appear.

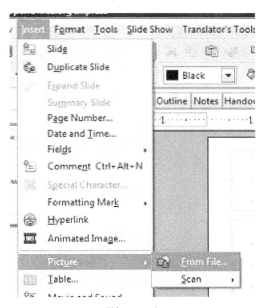

Figure 1

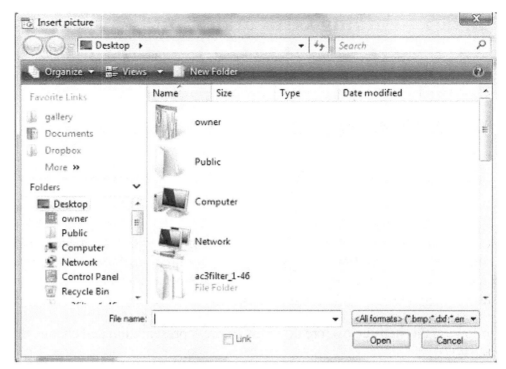

Figure 2

Step 3: Navigate to the location of the desired GIF and click on it. Once clicked, the name of the GIF will be displayed in the **File name** textbox.

Figure 3

Note – OpenOffice Impress does not come preloaded with any GIFs; however, many free GIF downloads are available at the following link: *http://www.gifs.net/gif/*

Step 4: Click **Open**. The GIF will be inserted into the presentation.

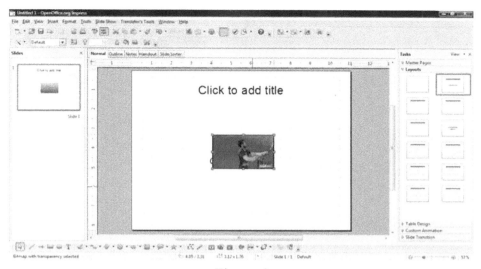

Figure 4

Step 5: Move the inserted GIF to the desired location within the slide. This is done by clicking anywhere within the GIF and dragging the GIF to the preferred location.

Adding Sounds

OpenOffice Impress also allows users to add sounds to a presentation. Similar to a GIF, adding sounds provides users with another technique for drawing attention to a presentation. The following steps outline how this is done.

Step 1: Click **Insert**, located on the Menu Bar.

Step 2: From the Insert drop-down menu, select **Movie and Sound**. The **Insert Movie and Sound** dialog box will appear.

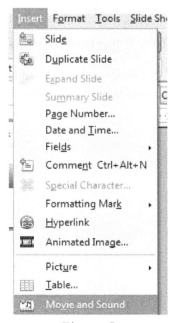

Figure 5

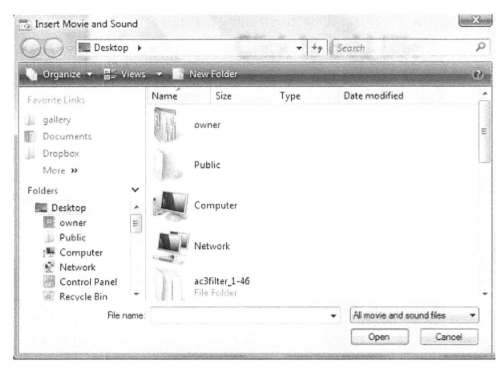

Figure 6

Step 3: Navigate to the location of the desired sound and click it. Once clicked, the name of the sound will be displayed in the **File name** textbox.

Figure 7

Note – OpenOffice Impress does not come preloaded with any sounds; however, many free sounds are available at the following link: *http://www.findsounds.com/*

Step 4: Click **Open**. The sound will be inserted into the presentation.

Note – The sound will play automatically when the presentation is shown in Slide Show view. The sound can also be played manually by clicking **Play** on the **Movie and Sound** toolbar.

Figure 8

Growth & Assessment

1. Why should sounds or GIFs be placed in the same folder as the presentation?

2. Does OpenOffice Impress come preloaded with any GIFs?

3. How is the Insert Movie and Sound dialog box opened?

4. Sounds can be added to a presentation.

   a. TRUE

   b. FALSE

Section 2.6 – Adding Animation

Section Objective:

- Learn how to add animations to slides.

Adding Animations

In OpenOffice Impress, animation refers to the movement and sound accompanying text or slides in a presentation. Adding animation to slides can often add excitement to the presentation by displaying text or an object at crucial moments. Adding animation also allows for smooth transitions between the topics covered in a presentation, which helps to create a more professional look.

Impress allows users to easily animate any object that has been placed into a presentation. Objects include, but are not limited to, images, charts, and text. The steps below explain how users can add animations to a presentation. Before following the steps below, create a slide with a blank layout and insert a piece of ClipArt.

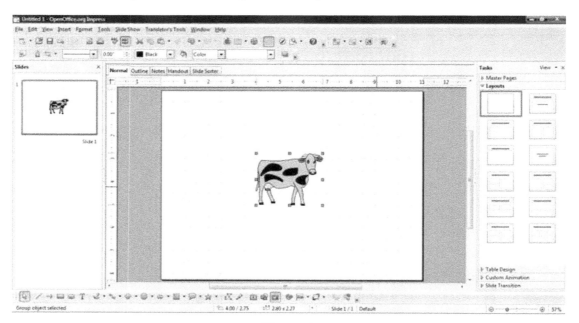

Figure 1

Step 1: Make sure that the previously created slide is selected and click on the piece of ClipArt that was added to the slide.

Step 2: Click on the **Custom Animation** tab, located on the **Tasks** pane, to expand the options available.

Figure 2

Step 3: Click the **Add...** button in the **Modify Effect** portion of the Tasks pane. The **Custom Animation** dialog box will appear.

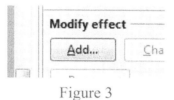

Figure 3

Figure 4

Step 4: Select one of the tabs located along the top of the dialog box. The tabs correspond to the time in which the animation takes place.

Note – The default tab in OpenOffice Impress is the **Entrance** tab.

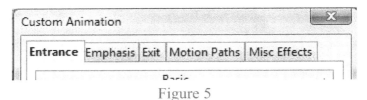

Figure 5

Step 5: Select the preferred animation from the options available.

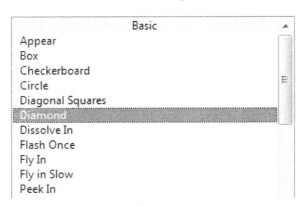

Figure 6

Step 6: In the **Speed** drop-down menu, users have the ability to select the speed at which the animation occurs.

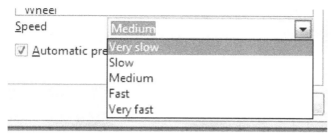

Figure 7

Step 7: Click **OK**. The new custom animation will be displayed in the **Custom Animation** pane.

Figure 8

Note – OpenOffice Impress allows users to make additional modifications to the custom animation directly from the **Custom Animation** pane. From the pane, the user has the ability to change when the animation starts, the direction in which it will move, and the speed of the animation.

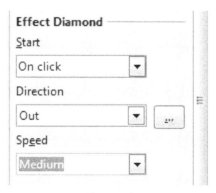

Figure 9

Growth & Assessment

1. What does animation refer to?

2. What objects can be animated in an Impress presentation?

3. The Custom Animation dialog box can be opened by clicking on the Add... button in the Modify Effect portion of the pane.

   a. TRUE

   b. FALSE

4. Where do users select the speed of the animation?

Section 2.7 – Editing Animations

Section Objectives:

- Learn how to reorder animations in slides.

- Learn how to remove animations in slides.

- Learn how to test the animations in slides.

Reorder, Remove, and Test Animations

In OpenOffice Impress, if there is more than one animation on a slide, the Custom Animation pane will list all of the animations being used. Impress allows users to control the order of the animations, remove animations, and test animations through the Custom Animation pane. This section will outline how to complete these tasks while working on a presentation.

Reordering Animations

Step 1: Create a new presentation, and add a slide with a blank layout.

Step 2: Enter text into the slide and create two animations for it.

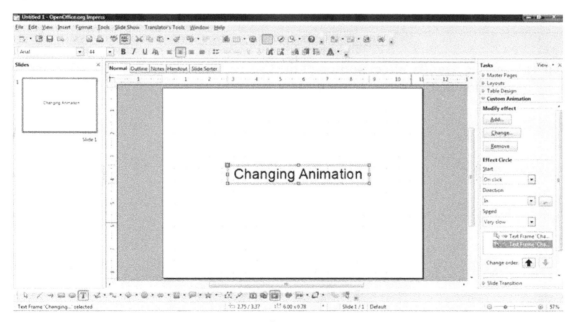

Figure 1

Step 3: Click the **Custom Animation** tab, located on the **Tasks** pane, to expand the options available.

Figure 2

Step 4: From the **Modify effect** portion of the Custom Animation pane list, select the first animation that was created for the text.

Figure 3

Step 5: Click the **Down Arrow** next to **Change Order** to move the first animation below the second animation. This will cause the order of the animations to change.

Figure 4

Removing Animations

As stated above, OpenOffice Impress allows users to remove an animation from a slide. Removing an animation can be done at any time while working on a slide. The following steps outline how this is done.

Note – Use the same slide as used in the steps above.

Step 1: Click the **Custom Animation** tab, located on the **Tasks** pane, to expand the options available.

Step 2: From the **Modify effect** portion of the Custom Animation pane list, select the second animation that was created for the text.

Step 3: Click **Remove**. The second animation that was created for the text will be removed from the Custom Animation pane.

Figure 5

As stated above, OpenOffice Impress allows users to test the animations in a slide. This is useful when a user is unsure of how an animation may look in the presentation, or when a user is trying to figure out the preferred speed of an animation. By testing animations, users can apply different effects to discover the preferred combination of animations that will best present the information on the slides.

Impress allows users to test the animations at any time while working on a slide. To do this, navigate to the **Custom Animation** tab located on the Tasks pane. At the bottom of the Custom Animation pane, click **Play**. The current animations applied to the slide will be displayed.

Figure 6

Growth & Assessment

1. If a user has more than one animation on a slide, they will see that the Custom Animation pane lists all of the animations that are in use on that slide.

    a. TRUE

    b. FALSE

2. Once an animation has been added to a slide, it can't be deleted.

    a. TRUE

    b. FALSE

3. What can be used to control the order of the animations in a presentation?

4. What is one way to make sure an inserted animation works?

Section 2.8 – Inserting Charts

Section Objective:

- Learn how to insert charts into slides.

Inserting Charts

OpenOffice Impress allows users to insert colorful, easy-to-read charts into the slides of a presentation. Charts provide an easy and organized way to display information and visually project trends and patterns to the audience. This section will explain how a user can incorporate charts into a presentation and modify the charts once they have been added to a slide.

Inserting a Chart into a Slide

Step 1: Create a new presentation and create a slide with a blank layout.

Step 2: Click **Insert**, located on the Menu Bar.

Step 3: From the Insert drop-down menu, select **Chart…**. A Column Chart will be inserted into the previously created slide.

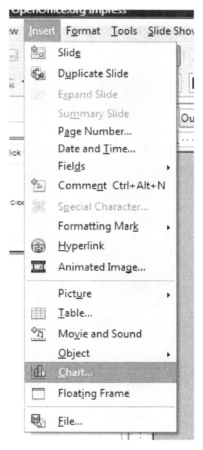

Figure 1

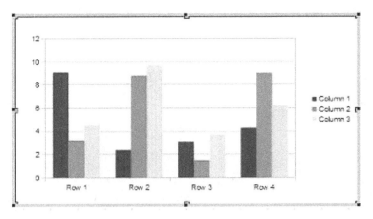

Figure 2

Note – By default, charts inserted into an Impress slide will automatically have sample data displayed within them.

Modifying the Chart Type

As stated above, Impress allows users to modify a chart once it has been inserted into a slide. The application, by default, will automatically insert a three bar Column Chart. The chart type can be modified to fit the user's preference and display the needed data. The following steps outline how this is done.

Step 1: Click on the chart that was inserted in the steps above. Once the chart has been clicked, make sure that the chart has handles displayed on each corner.

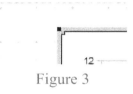

Figure 3

Step 2: Right-click anywhere within the chart area and select **Chart Type...**. The **Chart Type** dialog box will appear.

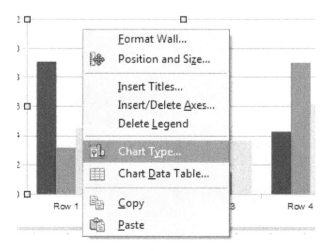

Figure 4

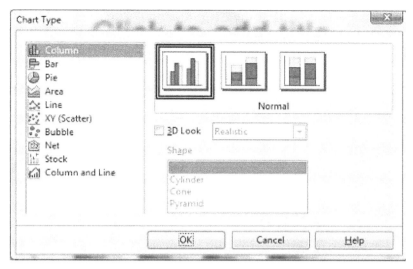

Figure 5

Step 3: Along the left-hand side of the Chart Type dialog box, there will be different categories of charts displayed. Select the desired chart type.

Step 4: Once the chart type has been selected, additional options for that type of chart will be displayed on the right side of the Chart Type dialog box. Select the desired chart options.

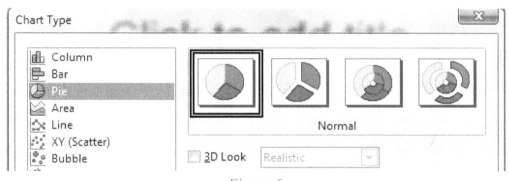

Figure 6

Step 5: Once the preferred chart has been selected, click **OK**.

Modifying the Chart Data

Once a chart has been added to a slide in an Impress presentation, the user not only has the ability to modify the chart type, but can also modify the chart data. The following steps outline how this is done.

Step 1: Click on the chart that has been inserted into the Impress presentation.

Step 2: Right-click anywhere within the chart area and select **Chart Data Table…**. The **Data Table** dialog box will appear.

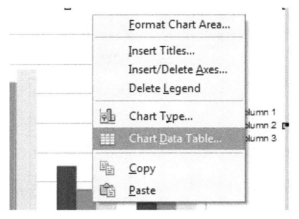

Figure 7

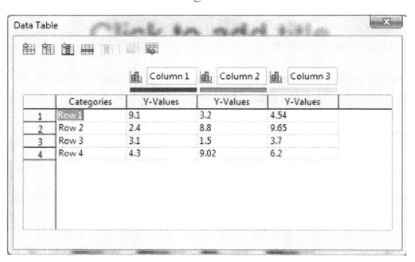

Figure 8

Step 3: Within the Chart Data Table dialog box, the user has the ability to modify the data. Add and/or remove columns and rows by using the buttons located along the top of the dialog box.

Note – Positioning the cursor over each button will display its functionality.

	Categories	Y-Values	Y-Values	Y-Values	
1	Q1	48	18	12	
2	Q2	454	923	828	
3	Q3	28	28	812	
4	Q4	102	822	182	

Figure 9

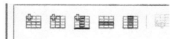

Figure 10

Growth & Assessment

1. What will Impress automatically insert as the default chart?

2. Impress does not add any default data into the chart when it is first created.

   a. TRUE

   b. FALSE

3. How is the Chart Type dialog box opened?

4. How is the Data Table dialog box opened?

Section 2.9 – Formatting Charts

Section Objective:

- Learn how to format a chart's Wall and Titles.

Formatting Charts

When a chart is inserted into an Impress presentation, by default the application will apply certain formatting to the chart. This is helpful because it allows the user to quickly create a chart for a presentation without having to worry about manually setting every format option. Once users become familiar with the application and are more comfortable creating charts, they may want to control the various formatting options rather than having the application do it for them. If this is the case, and a user would prefer to select the formatting options, Impress provides the necessary tools. This section will help users navigate through some of the application's formatting options for charts, such as formatting the Chart Wall and Chart Titles.

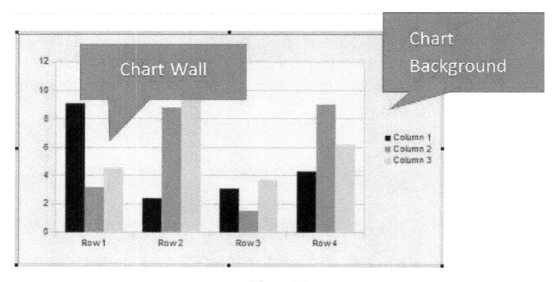

Figure X

Before following the steps below, create a new Impress presentation and insert a chart into any slide within the presentation.

Note – It is not necessary to format the data used. This section will only be working with visual formatting.

Step 1: Highlight the chart by clicking on the **Chart Wall**.

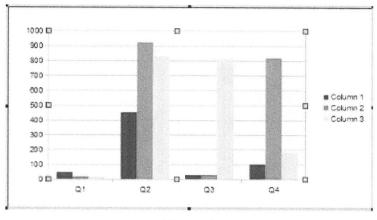

Figure 1

Step 2: Right-click on the highlighted chart to display the **Quick Menu**.

Step 3: From the Quick Menu, select **Format Wall…**. The **Chart Wall** dialog box will appear with the **Borders** tab selected.

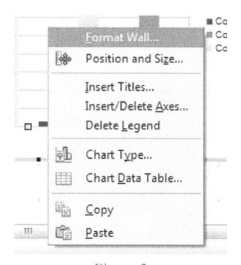

Figure 2

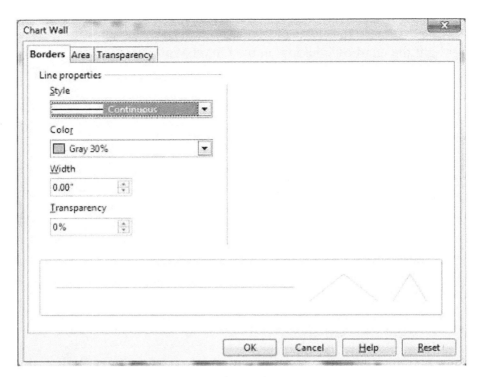

Figure 3

Step 4: The **Borders** tab allows users to set the style and width of the border that will be applied to the chart. For the purpose of this example, set the style as continuous and set the width to **.05**.

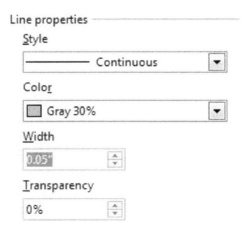

Figure 4

Step 5: The next tab in the dialog box is the **Area** tab. This tab allows users to set the background fill for the chart. For this example, select **Color** from the **Fill** drop-down menu, and select **Green**.

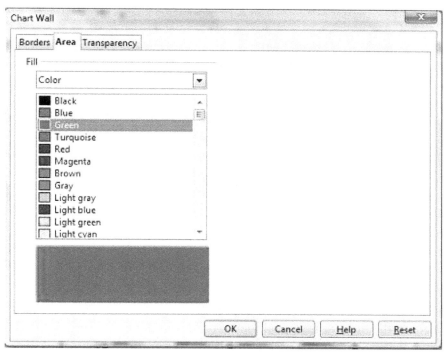

Figure 5

Step 6: The final tab in the **Chart Wall** dialog box is the **Transparency** tab. This tab allows the user to modify the background of the chart by adding a level of transparency, or by implementing a **Gradient**. For this example, set the gradient to **Ellipsoid**.

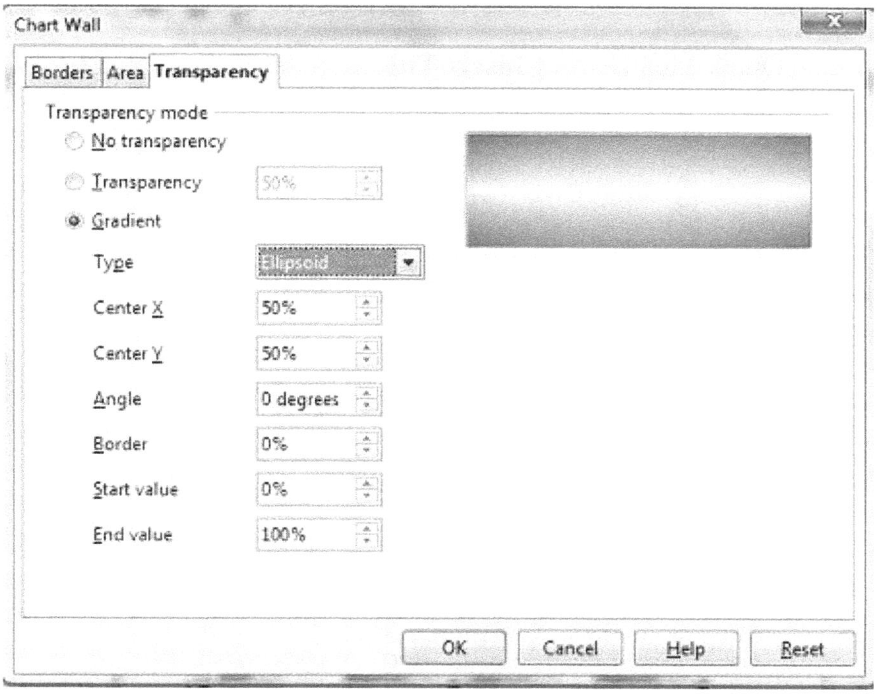

Figure 6

Step 7: Click **OK**. The changes will be applied to the Chart Wall.

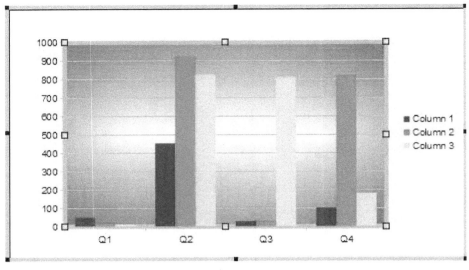

Figure 7

Formatting Chart Titles

Adding **Chart Titles** can be helpful when presenting unfamiliar charts to an audience. By displaying a chart title, the audience will better understand the meaning of the chart contents. Impress allows users to not only create a title for the inserted chart, but also provides X and Y axis labels which allow the user to add more information to the chart. The following steps outline how a user can access and utilize these formatting options.

Step 1: Highlight the chart by clicking on the **Chart Wall**.

Step 2: Right-click on the highlighted chart to display the **Quick Menu**.

Step 3: From the Quick Menu, select **Insert Titles…**. The **Titles** dialog box will appear.

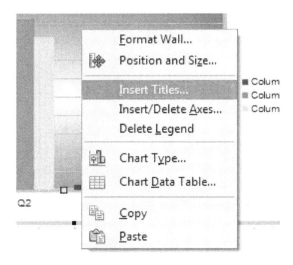

Figure 8

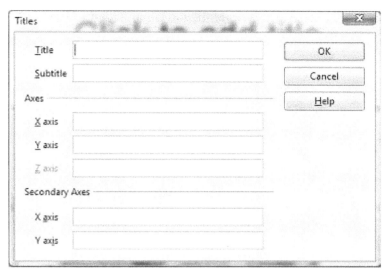

Figure 9

Step 4: The first two textboxes in the dialog box are where the user enters the chart name. For this example, enter "**Lesson 9**" into the **Title** textbox and "**Sample Chart**" into the **Subtitle** textbox.

Title	Lesson 9
Subtitle	Sample Chart

Figure 10

Step 5: The next section of the dialog box is where the user can enter labels for the X-axis and Y-axis of the chart. For this example, enter "**Product**" into the X-**axis** textbox and "**Number Sold**" into the **Y-axis** textbox.

Axes

X axis	Product
Y axis	Number Sold
Z axis	

Figure 11

Step 6: Click **OK**. The created titles and labels will be added to the chart.

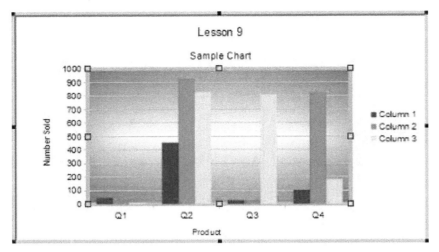

Figure 12

Growth & Assessment

1. What does the Borders tab do?

2. What does the Area tab do?

3. How does the Transparency tab let users alter the background of the chart?

4. Impress provides the tools that are needed to format every item contained within a chart.

   a. TRUE

   b. FALSE

Section 2.10 – Inserting Tables into Slides

Section Objective:

- Learn how to insert tables into slides.

Inserting Tables

Inserting a table into an OpenOffice Impress slide is a useful feature when presenting data. Tables allow users to better organize and display data for an audience. Impress will automatically increase or decrease the size of the table's cells, depending on its content. This feature is also useful because it saves the user from having to manually adjust the table when adding additional information. The following steps explain how a user can insert a table into an Impress slide.

Step 1: Create a new Impress presentation and place the insertion point inside the data portion of the Title slide.

Step 2: Click **Insert**, located on the Menu Bar.

Step 3: From the **Insert** drop-down menu, select **Table…**. The **Table** dialog box will appear.

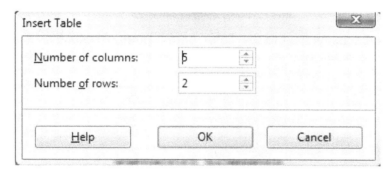

Figure 1

Step 4: Within the Size portion of the dialog box, select the table size by choosing the number of Columns and Row. Users can use the nudge buttons to select the table size, or type the values in manually.

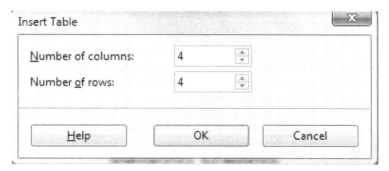

Figure 2

Step 5: Click **OK**. A blank table will be inserted into the slide.

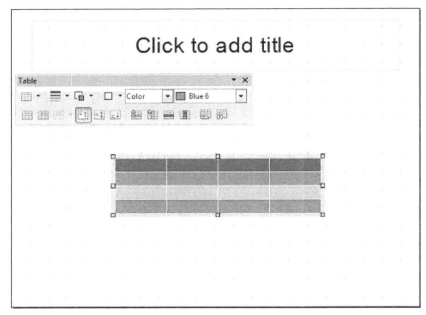

Figure 3

Users can also insert a table into a slide by using the **Drag Method**. The Drag Method allows users to quickly insert a blank table into any Impress presentation. To use the Drag Method, follow the steps below.

Step 1: Place the insertion point where the table is to appear.

Step 2: Click on the arrow next to the **Table** button on the Toolbar.

Figure 4

Step 3: A grid will appear on the screen. Select the preferred table size by dragging the cursor over the table grid. Once the preferred number of grids is selected, click the left mouse button. An empty table will appear in the Impress slide and the user can begin inserting data.

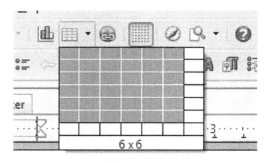

Figure 5

Growth & Assessment

1. Why would a user need to insert a table into an Impress slide?

2. In Impress users need to manually increase or decrease the size of the table's cells, depending on its content.

   a. TRUE

   b. FALSE

3. When creating a table, how are the number of Columns and Rows selected?

4. Explain how the Drag Method is used.

Section 2.11 – Duplicating, Deleting, and Moving Slides

Section Objective:

- Learn how to duplicate, delete, and move slides.

Duplicating, Deleting, and Moving Slides

OpenOffice Impress allows users to modify the order of a presentation by duplicating, deleting, and moving slides. This section will explain how to complete these three different types of modifications in an Impress presentation.

Duplicating Slides

Duplicating slides allows users to use a previously customized slide as a template for future slides. This saves users time and helps maintain a consistent look throughout a presentation. The following steps outline how this is done.

Note – Depending on the presentation, the text, graphics, animations, and multimedia may need to be changed from slide to slide.

Step 1: From inside the **Slides** pane, located on the left side of the Impress window, select the first slide of the presentation.

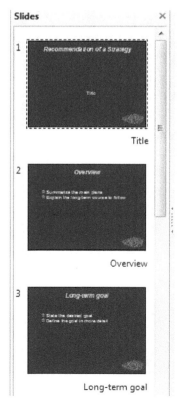

Figure 1

Step 2: Click **Insert**, located on the Menu Bar.

Step 3: From the Insert drop-down menu, click on **Duplicate Slide**. An exact duplicate, with all of the formatting and content from the original slide, will be inserted directly below the slide currently selected.

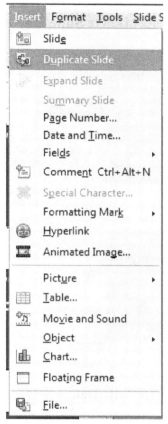

Figure 2

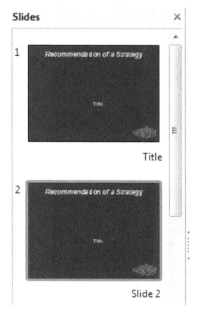

Figure 3

As stated above, Impress allows users to delete slides in a presentation. The following steps outline how this is done.

Step 1: Right-click on the desired slide. The Quick Menu will appear.

Step 2: From the Quick Menu, select **Delete Slide**. The selected slide will be deleted from the presentation.

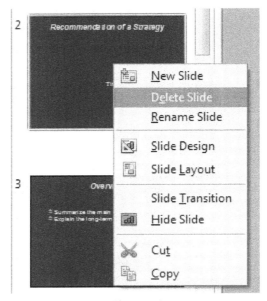

Figure 4

Note – Users can also select **Edit Delete Slide**, to delete an Impress slide from a presentation.

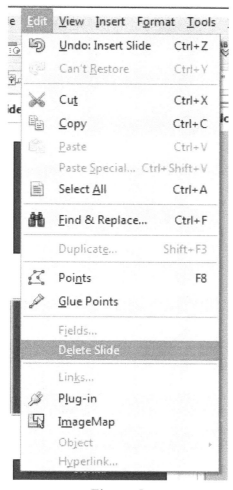

Figure 5

Moving Slides

At times, users may want to change the order of the slides in a presentation. This may be because a different order will better organize the presentation and display the information in a more logical way. OpenOffice Impress allows users to reorder the slides by moving them in the Slides pane. The following steps explain this in greater detail.

Step 1: Click on the preferred slide in the **Slides** pane.

Step 2: Click and hold the left mouse button on the selected slide.

Step 3: Drag the slide either forwards or backwards in the presentation's slide order to its intended location. There will be a dark line highlighting where the slide will be inserted once the mouse button is released.

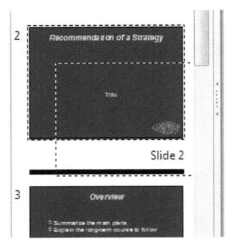

Figure 6

Step 4: Once the slide is in the desired position, release the left mouse button. The slide will be dropped into its new location.

Growth & Assessment

1. Duplicating slides allows users to create one slide and customize it, and then make duplicate slides and only change the text, graphics, animations, and multimedia, as necessary.

   a. TRUE

   b. FALSE

2. Within which menu is Duplicate Slide located?

3. What happens when Duplicate Slide is selected?

4. How is the slide order of a presentation changed from the Slides pane?

Section 2.12 – Inserting Slides from Other Presentations

Section Objective:

- Learn how to insert slides from other presentations.

Inserting Slides from Other Presentations

The benefit of having many different presentations is the ability to pull slides from one presentation and add them to another. OpenOffice Impress allows users to perform this type of action and the steps below outline how it can be done.

Before following the steps below, create a simple one slide presentation which will be used to copy information from. Enter "**Other Presentation**" into the Title slide textbox, and save it to the Desktop as "**Sample**."

Step 1: Create a new Impress presentation using the **Introducing a New Product** template. In the **Slides** pane, click the second slide.

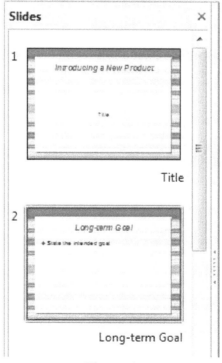

Figure 1

Step 2: Click **Insert**, located on the Menu Bar.

Step 3: From the Insert drop-down menu, select **File…**. The **Insert File** dialog box will appear.

Figure 2

Step 4: Navigate to the "**Sample**" presentation created at the beginning of the section and then click **Open**. The **Insert Slides/Objects** window will open.

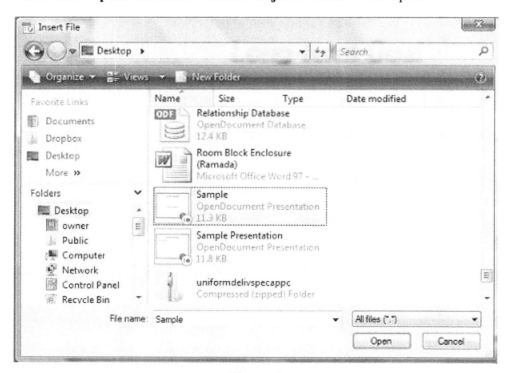

Figure 3

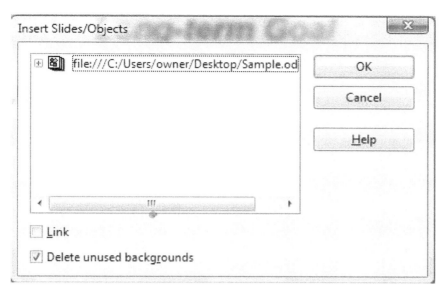

Figure 4

Step 5: Click on the plus sign next to the file name to expand the presentation to display all of the slides available.

Figure 5

Step 6: Click the **OK** button. The slide(s) that are selected will be placed below the currently selected slide in the presentation.

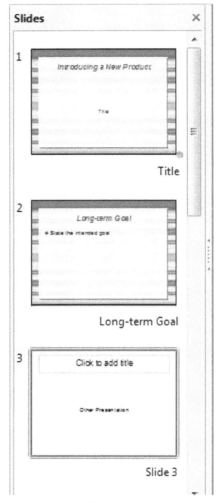

Figure 6

Growth & Assessment

1. Why re-use slides from a previous presentation?

2. Users can move a slide from a previous presentation into one that is currently being worked on.

   a. TRUE

   b. FALSE

3. How is the Insert File dialog box opened from the Insert drop-down menu?

4. When inserting new slides into an existing Impress document, where are the new slides placed?

Section 2.13 – Adding an Interaction Button

Section Objective:

- Learn how to add an interaction button.

Adding an Interaction Button

Interactions allow users to assign links to button shapes that have been added to a presentation, and then assign them an action that will occur when the button is clicked. Some examples of the type of actions that can occur when a button is activated are: sounds, external links to web pages, and links to different slides in the presentation. This section will cover a series of steps which will outline how an interaction button is added to a presentation.

Before following the steps below, view the table below listing the different interactions available in OpenOffice Impress.

Interaction Name	Object Needed as a Target
Go to Previous Slide	N/A
Go to Next Slide	N/A
Go to First Slide	N/A
Go to Last Slide	N/A
Go to Page or Object	Choose a target from the list in the Target box. The user can search for a specific target in the Document box at the bottom of the window.
Go to Document	Select the document in the Document box. Use the Browse button to open a file selection dialog box.
Play Sound	Select the sound file containing the sound to be played. Use the Browse button to open a file selection dialog box to find the file.
Run program	Select the program to run. Use the Browse button to locate it.
Run Macro	Select a macro that will run during the presentation. Use the Browse button provided to open the Macro Browser dialog box.
Exit Presentation	When the user clicks the image or text, the Slide Show will end and the Impress presentation window will once again be displayed.

The following steps explain how to add an interaction button to a presentation by following a specific example. The following steps explain how to add an image with an interaction, to a slide.

Step 1: Create a new Impress presentation and insert a slide with a blank layout.

Step 2: Click **Tools**, located on the Menu Bar.

Step 3: From the Tools drop-down menu, select **Gallery**. The **Gallery** pane will appear on the application window.

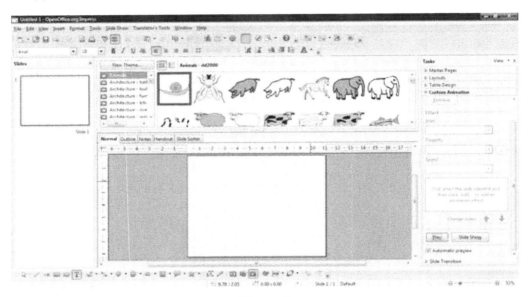

Figure 1

Step 4: From the available themes in the gallery, select the **Arrows** theme. The available arrow images will appear.

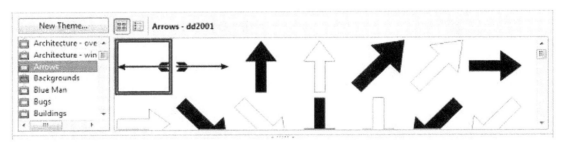

Figure 2

Step 5: Click and drag an arrow onto the slide. When the arrow is positioned over the slide let go of the left mouse button and the arrow will be inserted into the slide.

Figure 3

Step 6: Click **Slide Show**, located on the Menu Bar.

Step 7: From the Slide Show drop-down menu, select **Interactions...**. The **Interactions** dialog box will appear.

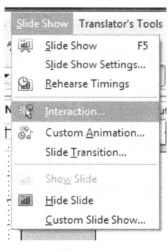

Figure 4

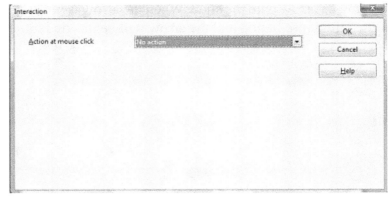

Figure 5

Step 8: In the **Action at Mouse Click** drop-down menu, the user is able to select the preferred action that will take place when the image is clicked. Select the preferred action and click **OK**.

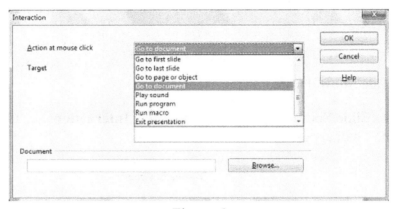

Figure 6

Step 9: Once OK has been clicked, the interaction will be added to the arrow image. When running the slide show, click on the arrow to cause the action to occur.

Growth & Assessment

1. What do Interaction buttons do?

2. In order for a sound interaction button to work, the target must first be linked with what?

3. Some of the actions that happen when an Action Button is clicked are: sounds, linking to a web page, or moving to a different slide within the presentation

    a. TRUE

    b. FALSE

4. If clicking a target takes the user to another document, what is the name of the interaction used?

Section 2.14 – Inserting Slide Numbers and the Time and Date

Section Objectives:

- Learn how to insert slide numbers into slides.

- Learn how to insert the date and time into slides.

OpenOffice Impress allows users to add slide numbers to a presentation. Slide numbers are useful for the user, as well as the audience when referencing back to specific slides. Impress also allows users to add the time and date to the presentation slides. Both the slide number, and the time and date can also be set up to automatically appear on the Impress slides. This section will explain how to add these useful features to a presentation.

Inserting Slide Numbers

Step 1: Create a new Impress presentation with the first slide being the Title slide followed by five blank slides. Once this has been done, select the Title slide.

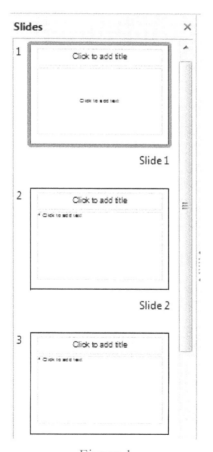

Figure 1

Step 2: Click **Insert**, located on the Menu Bar.

Step 3: From the Insert drop-down menu, select **Page Number…**. The **Headers and Footers** dialog box will appear with the **Slide** tab selected.

Figure 2

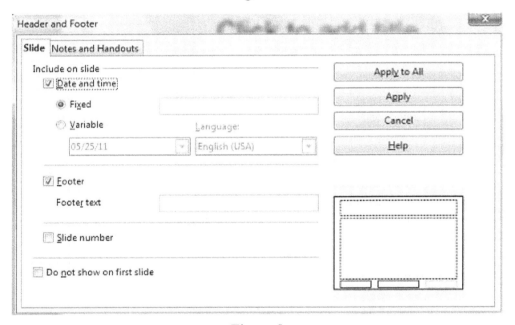

Figure 3

Step 4: Check the checkbox next to **Slide Number**.

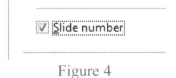

Figure 4

Step 5: Click **Apply** to add the page number to the selected slide, or click **Apply to All** to add the page number to all slides in the presentation. For this particular example, click **Apply to All**. Page numbers will be inserted into the bottom right-hand corner of every slide in the presentation.

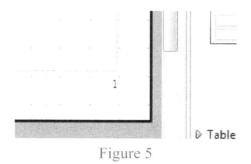

Figure 5

Note – If a slide number isn't needed on the first slide of the presentation, check the checkbox next to **Do Not Show on First Slide**.

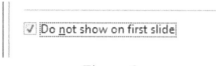

Figure 6

Inserting the Date and Time

Note – The Date and Time will always appear in the bottom left corner of an Impress slide.

Step 1: Use the same presentation as used in the steps above and select the first slide in the presentation.

Step 2: Click **Insert**, located on the Menu Bar.

Step 3: From the Insert drop-down menu, select **Date and Time**. The **Headers and Footers** dialog box will appear with the **Slide** tab selected.

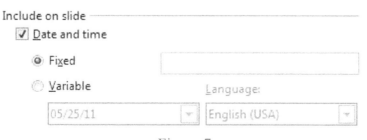

Figure 7

Step 4: Check the checkbox next to **Date and Time**.

Figure 8

Step 5: Click the radio button next to **Fixed** or **Variable** depending on the type of date and time style preferred (refer to the style descriptions below). For this example select **Fixed** and type **1/1/2000** into the textbox.

Date and Time Styles:

- **Fixed** – If a user selects this style they will need to manually enter how they want the date and time to appear on the screen. What the user types into the textbox will be inserted into each slide and will not change unless the user manually re-enters the date and time.

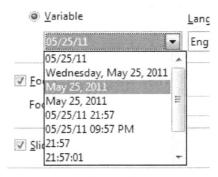

Figure 9

- **Variable** – If a user selects this style, they will choose from a variety of date and time styles that the application provides in a drop-down menu. The date and time that will be inserted into the slides will be constantly updated to reflect the current date and time.

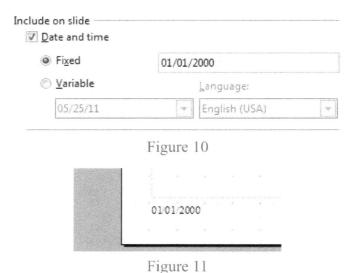

Figure 10

Figure 11

Step 6: Click **Apply** to add the date and time only to the selected slide, or click **Apply to All** to add the date and time to all slides in the presentation. For this particular example, click **Apply to All**. The previously entered date and time will be inserted into the bottom left-hand corner of every slide in the presentation.

Note – If the Date and Time isn't needed on the first slide of the presentation, check the checkbox next to **Do Not Show on First Slide**.

Growth & Assessment

1. Users can use the tools that Impress provides to automate the entering of what two pieces of data?

2. The Slide Number checkbox is found on the Slide tab of what dialog box?

3. If a user doesn't want a slide number displayed on the first page of the presentation, they can check the checkbox next to Apply to All.

   a. TRUE

   b. FALSE

4. If Variable style is selected, the date and time inserted into the slides will be constantly updated to reflect the current date and time.

   a. TRUE

   b. FALSE

Section 2.15 – Viewing Slides in Black and White or Grayscale

Section Objective:

- Learn how to view slides in black and white or grayscale.

View Slides in Black and White or Grayscale

Presentations can become very colorful, especially when the user customizes the background, adds tables and charts, and illustrations. OpenOffice Impress allows users to change the color of a presentation to view the slides in Black and White or Grayscale if the colors of a presentation become too overwhelming. This section will explain how to a user can change the color of a presentation to view the slides in Black and White or Grayscale.

Before following the steps below, create a new Impress presentation using the **Recommendation of a Strategy** template. The presentation will open in full color.

Viewing a Presentation in Black and White

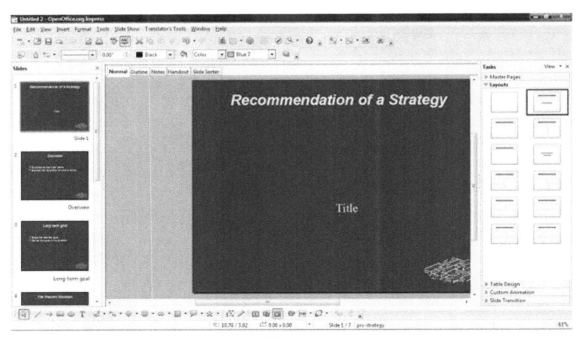

Figure 1

Step 1: Click **View**, located on the Menu Bar.

Step 2: From the View drop-down menu, select **Color/Grayscale**, and then click **Black and White**. The slides will change from color to black and white.

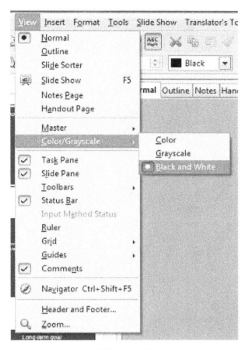

Figure 2

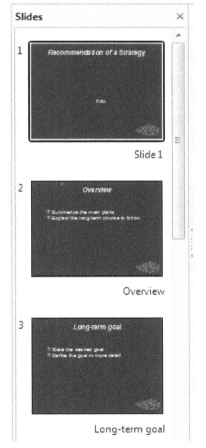

Figure 3

Note – The user can view the slides in color at any time by going back to the View drop-down menu, selecting Color/Grayscale, and then clicking **Color**.

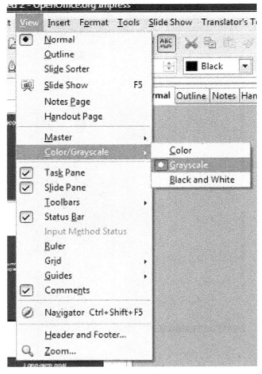

Figure 4

Viewing a Presentation in Grayscale

As stated above, Impress allows users to also view a presentation in Grayscale. Viewing a presentation in Grayscale will cause the slides to display in different hues of grey and white. The following steps outline how a user can view a presentation in Grayscale.

Step 1: Using the same presentation as used in the steps above, click **View**, located on the Menu Bar.

Step 2: From the View drop-down menu, select **Color/Grayscale**, and then click **Grayscale**. This will cause the slides to change from Black and White to varied shades of gray.

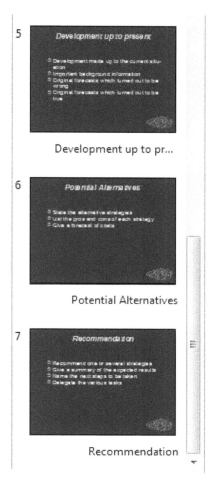

Figure 5

Growth & Assessment

1. How is grayscale different from black and white?

2. Color/Grayscale is found under what menu?

3. Selecting Black and White from the View drop-down menu will change the slides to Grayscale.

   a. TRUE

   b. FALSE

4. Users can view the slide's color at any time by going back to Color/Grayscale, in the View drop-down menu, and selecting Black and White.

   a. TRUE

   b. FALSE

Unit Three

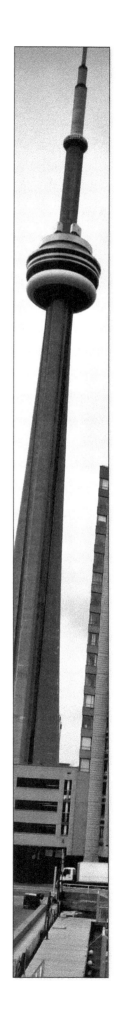

Section 3.1 – Adding a Background

Section Objective:

- Learn how to add a background.

Adding a Background

OpenOffice Impress allows users to add backgrounds to make presentations more visually appealing. Impress provides users with different background templates which can be used to quickly apply a background to a presentation. Impress also allows users to add a custom background if the templates are not desired. The following steps outline how this is done.

Step 1: Create a new Impress presentation.

Step 2: Select the Title slide in the presentation.

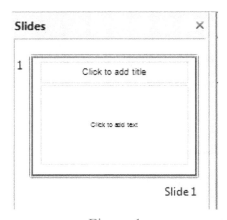

Figure 1

Step 3: Click **Format**, located on the Menu Bar.

Step 4: From the Format drop-down menu, click **Page…**. The **Page Setup** dialog box will appear.

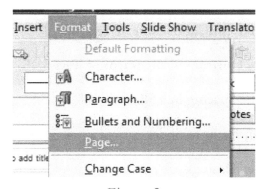

Figure 2

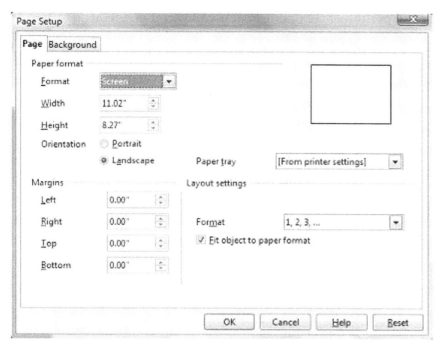

Figure 3

Step 5: Click on the **Background** tab located at the top of the Page Setup dialog box. This will cause the **Background** dialog box to open.

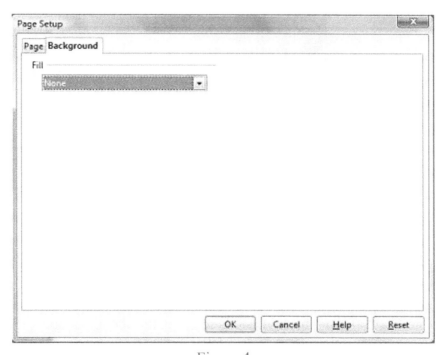

Figure 4

Step 6: In the **Fill** portion of the dialog box, use the drop-down menu to select the preferred **Fill Type**. The available Fill Types are described in the table below.

Fill Type	Description
None	This will cause no background to be displayed.
Color	This fill type will be a solid color that can be selected from the options provided.
Gradient	This fill type offers several colored backgrounds that have effects such as blank edges, fading, etc…
Hatching	This fill type offers different textured backgrounds.
Bitmap	This fill type allows users to insert a picture to use as the background.

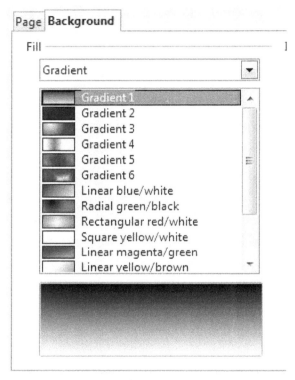

Figure 5

Note – Depending on the option selected in the Fill drop-down menu, there may be additional options displayed on the right side of the Background dialog box. These options can be used to customize the backgrounds provided by the application. For example, if a **Hatching** background is selected, the additional options will allow the user to choose the color shown in the background of the pattern.

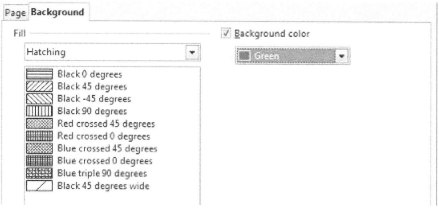

Figure 6

Step 7: Once the preferred Fill Type has been selected, click **OK**. A pop up window will appear asking if the selected background should be added to all of the slides in the presentation. If the user clicks **Yes**, the selected background will be applied to all of the slides. If the user clicks **No**, the selected background will only be added to the current slide. Click **Yes** or **No** to apply the background to the desired slide(s).

Figure 7

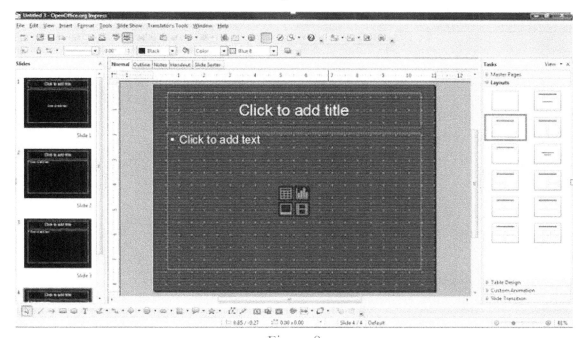

Figure 8

Note – Remove the background from a presentation by navigating to the **Background** dialog box and select **None** from the Fill drop-down menu.

Growth & Assessment

1. What does the Bitmap Fill Type allow users to do?

2. OpenOffice Impress allows users to add different backgrounds.

   a. TRUE

   b. FALSE

3. Why would a background be added to a presentation?

Section 3.2 – Customizing a Background

Section Objective:

- Learn how to customize the presentation background.

Customizing a Background

OpenOffice Impress allows users to apply different backgrounds to a presentation. This is useful when a specific style is needed to appeal to a particular audience. Impress allows users to modify the background's color, gradient, and texture, as well as add a bitmap (picture) to the background. Below is a list describing the different background categories available for the user to modify.

Background Categories:

- **Color** – Offers the user a wide array of background color options.

- **Gradient** – A gradient is a shift in color. For example, Gradient 1 shifts from black to white, beginning at the top of the slide.

- **Hatching** – Hatches are a series of lines. They run vertical, horizontal, and diagonal in a series of patterns.

- **Bitmap** – Bitmaps are pictures that can be inserted into a presentation to use as a background.

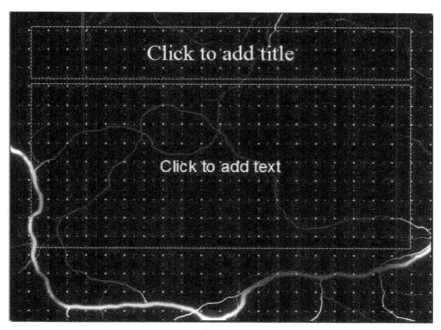

Figure 1

Step 1: Create a new Impress presentation and select a slide to customize.

Step 2: Click anywhere within the main text area of the slide so that it is highlighted.

Figure 2

Step 3: Click **Format**, located on the Menu Bar.

Step 4: From the Format drop-down menu, select **Area...**. The **Area** dialog box will appear with the **Area** tab selected.

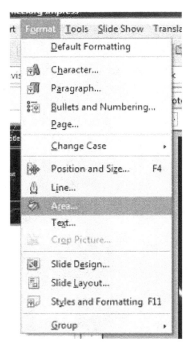

Figure 3

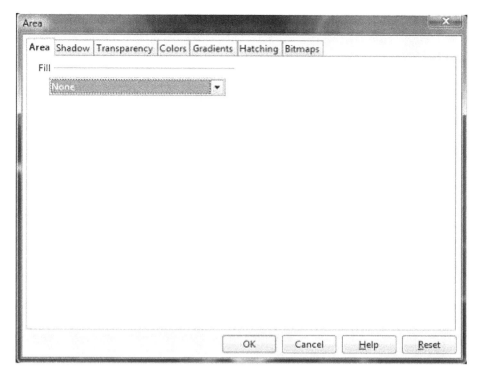

Figure 4

Step 5: From the **Fill** drop-down menu, select the preferred fill type which will be used to modify the background.

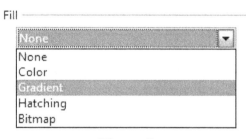

Figure 5

Step 6: Once the preferred fill type has been selected, additional options will be displayed on the right side of the dialog box. These options can be used to customize the selected background. Depending on the fill type selected, the user has the ability to modify the background's color, gradient, and texture, as well as add a bitmap to use as the background. Once the desired options have been selected, click **OK**. The new modifications will be applied to the background of the selected slide.

Figure 6

Growth & Assessment

1. OpenOffice Impress allows a user to insert different backgrounds into a presentation.

   a. TRUE

   b. FALSE

2. Depending upon the fill type selected, how many aspects of the background can the user modify?

3. What are the background fill categories?

4. What are Hatches?

Section 3.3 – Accessing Color and Fill Options

Section Objective:

- Learn how to access color and fill options.

Accessing Color and Fill Options

All objects in OpenOffice Impress can be filled with any color provided by the application. Palettes, which can be accessed through the Format drop-down menu, allow users to not only apply basic colors, but basic gradients and textures as well. By using palettes to modify the presentation's appearance, users can create a completely unique presentation.

Step 1: Create a new Impress presentation and select one of the textboxes on the Title slide.

Step 2: Click **Format**, located on the Menu Bar.

Step 3: From the Format drop-down menu, select **Areas…**. The **Area** dialog box will appear with the **Area** tab selected.

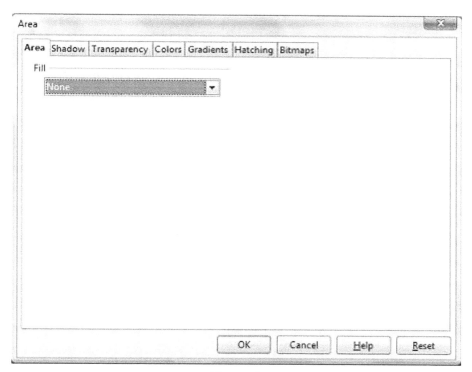

Figure 1

Step 4: Click the **Colors** tab, located at the top of the Area dialog box, to display the **Color** dialog box.

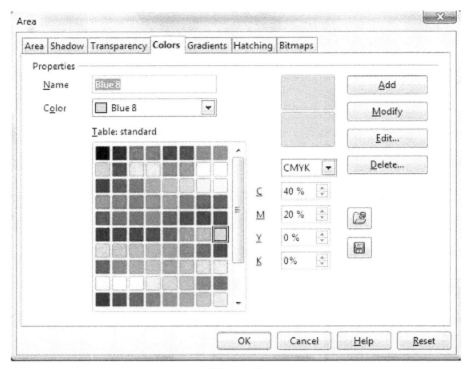

Figure 2

Step 5: Click on the **Fill Color** pull-down menu to display the available color options. Select the preferred color for the selected slide.

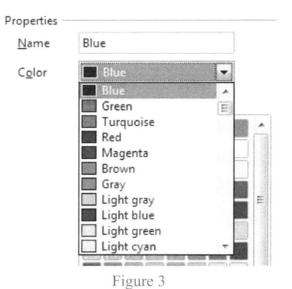

Figure 3

In OpenOffice Impress, if a user doesn't want any of the color options available in the Fill Color pull-down menu, more colors can be found by following the steps below.

Step 1: Select the same textbox that was worked on in the steps above.

Step 2: Click **Format**, located on the Menu Bar.

Step 3: From the Format drop-down menu, select **Areas…**. The Area dialog box will appear with the **Fill** tab selected.

Step 4: Click the **Colors** tab to display the Color pane. On the Color pane, click **Edit…**. A separate **Color** dialog box will appear.

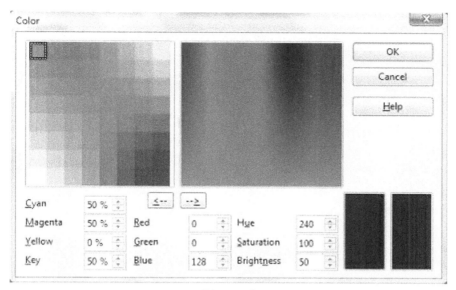

Figure 4

Step 5: The Custom Colors palate will be displayed on the right side of the dialog box. Use the cursor to drag the small box across the color palate to find the preferred color. Once the color has been selected, click OK. The new color will appear in the selected textbox.

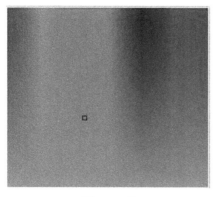

Figure 5

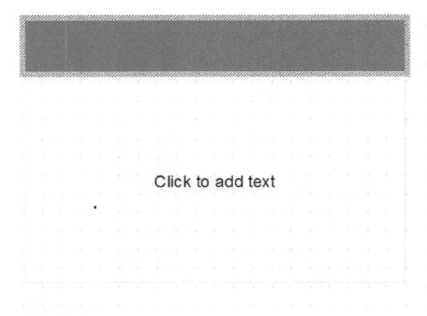

Figure 6

Growth & Assessment

1. Where is the palette located?

2. Textboxes can be filled with color.

   a. TRUE

   b. FALSE

3. Aside from basic colors, what other fill features can be accessed from the palette?

Section 3.4 – Using the Outline Tab

Section Objective:

- Learn how to use the outline tab.

The Outline Tab

There are several ways to view a presentation in OpenOffice Impress. One available view, which can be accessed by clicking the Outline tab located in the Slides pane, is the Outline view. The Outline view displays the slide titles and the main text within each of the slides. The main text for each slide is indented and displayed below the corresponding slide title.

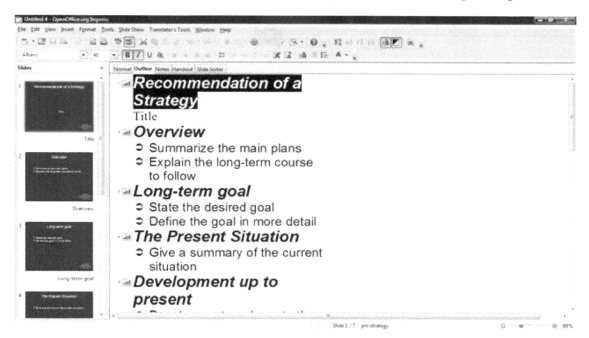

Figure 1

When a user is working in the Outline view, it is easy to view the text for an entire presentation. The Outline view also makes it easy to rearrange points, move slides from one position to another, and format the slides. The following steps outline how a user can access the Outline view and make similar modifications to a presentation.

Step 1: Create a new Impress presentation.

Step 2: At the top of the **Slides** pane, located on the left side of the application window, select the **Outline** tab. The **Outline** view will replace the Normal view on the Slide pane.

Figure 2

Now that the presentation is being viewed as an outline, the user has the ability to adjust which information is displayed. If a user wants to only view the slide titles, the main text for each slide can be collapsed. Collapsing the main text, or sub-heading, for each slide title can be done by double-clicking the **Outline** icon located next to each slide title, or main heading.

Note – Double-clicking the icon a second time will cause all of the slide sub-headings to reappear.

Figure 3

Growth & Assessment

1. There are several ways to view a presentation in OpenOffice Impress.

    a. TRUE

    b. FALSE

2. What happens when a user double-clicks the Outline icon?

3. What happens when a user double-clicks the Outline icon twice?

Section 3.5 – Working with Text and Paragraphs in Outline View

Section Objective:

- Learn how to work with text and paragraphs in outline view.

Working with Text and Paragraphs in Outline View

OpenOffice Impress allows users to modify the text while working on a presentation in the Outline view. When the Outline tab has been selected, a textual outline of the presentation will appear in the Slide pane. Here, the user can change the text within the presentation, as well as move the text to a different position on the outline by promoting, demoting, and/or moving it up or down. This section will explain how all of these modifications can be made to the text while working in the Outline view.

This first set of steps will explain how to change the look of the text while working in the Outline View.

Step 1: Create a new Impress presentation using the **Introducing a New Product** template. In the outline, select the text under **Fulfilling Customer Needs**.

Fulfilling Customer Needs

- Describe the main attributes of the product
- Link the product attributes to customer needs

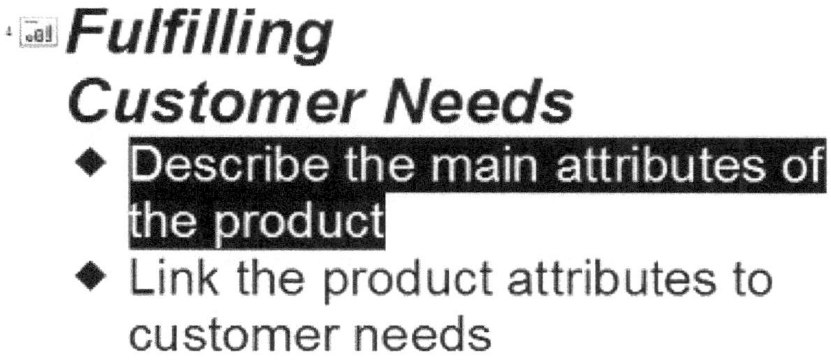

Figure 1

Step 2: Click **Format**, located on the Menu Bar.

Step 3: From the Format drop-down menu, select **Character…**. The **Character** dialog box will appear and display the necessary tools for modifying the text. Use the tools within the dialog box to make the desired changes to the text.

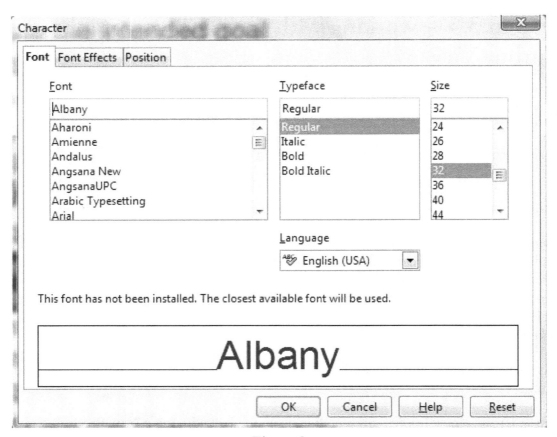

Figure 2

Note – The text can also be modified by using the buttons located on the **Formatting Toolbar**.

Figure 3

As stated above, Impress allows users to position paragraphs, or a line of text, in an outline by promoting, demoting, and/or moving it up or down. A description of each option is provided below.

- **Promoting Paragraphs** – When a user promotes a paragraph in an outline, the paragraph will move to the left.

- **Demoting Paragraphs** – When a user demotes a paragraph in an outline, the paragraph will move to the right.

- **Moving a Paragraph Up** – When a user moves a paragraph up, the application exchanges it with the paragraph or line of text above.

- **Moving a Paragraph Down** – When a user moves a paragraph down, the application will exchange it with the paragraph or line of text below.

Steps for Promoting/Demoting a Paragraph:

Step 1: Select the desired paragraph or line of text that will be moved.

Step 2: Click on the **Left Arrow** or **Right Arrow** on the toolbar to promote or demote the paragraph within the slide.

> **Note** – Impress allows users to demote text as many as **10** levels if the original text was a level **1** heading.

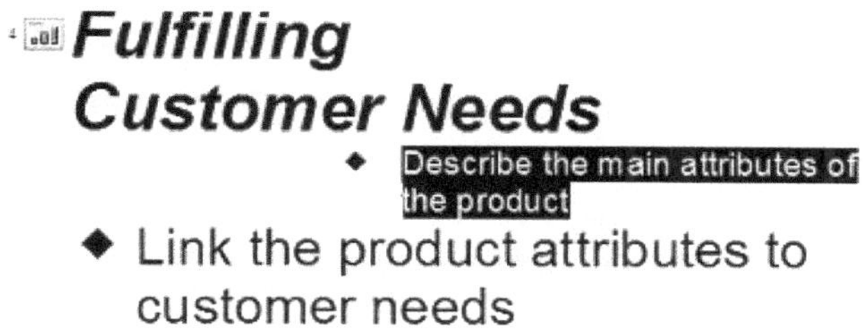
Fulfilling
Customer Needs
Describe the main attributes of the product
Link the product attributes to customer needs

Figure 4

Steps for Moving a Paragraph Up/Down:

Step 1: Select the desired paragraph or line of text that will be moved.

Step 2: Click the **Up Arrow** or **Down Arrow** on the toolbar to move the information up or down the slide, or to an entirely new slide.

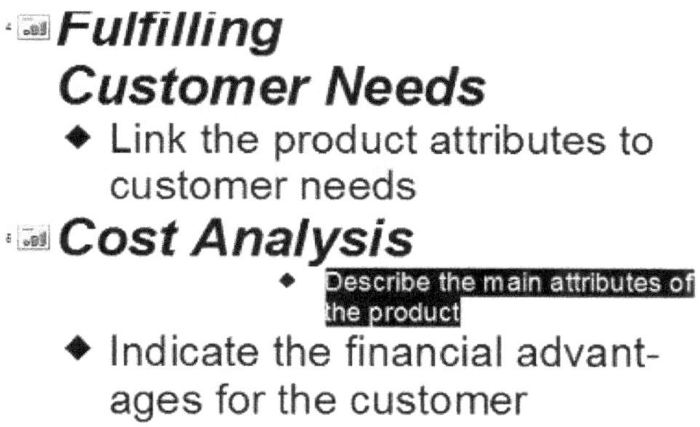
Fulfilling
Customer Needs
Link the product attributes to customer needs
Cost Analysis
Describe the main attributes of the product
Indicate the financial advant-ages for the customer

Figure 5

Growth & Assessment

1. The Promote and Demote options allow a user to move the text.

   a. TRUE

   b. FALSE

2. After selecting the line of text, what are the Up and Down Arrows used for?

3. Where are the Promote and Demote icons found?

Section 3.6 – Printing an Outline

Section Objective:

- Learn how to print an outline.

Printing an Outline

After creating an outline in OpenOffice Impress, the application allows users to print it. A printed outline is a useful tool when a user wants to organize information for an audience. By distributing printed outlines to the audience, it allows the people viewing the presentation to follow along, and it provides them with a document they can refer to once the presentation has ended.

In Impress, an outline will print all of the information shown in the Outline view; therefore, it is important that users format the text in the outline before printing. The following steps explain how a user can print an outline; however, before beginning the steps below, create a new Impress presentation using the **Introducing a New Product** template so that there are multiple levels in the outline.

Figure 1

Step 1: Click the **Outline Tab**, located along the top of the Slide pane, to change the view of the presentation to **Outline View**.

Figure 2

Step 2: For this example, print the outline so that all of the levels within the outline are shown. This can be done by double-clicking the Outline icon next to each collapsed sub-heading. Once every sub-heading is visible, move to the next step.

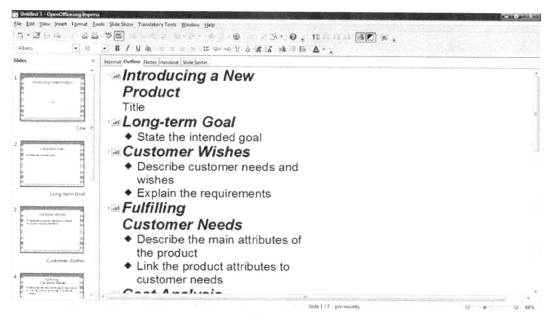

Figure 3

Step 3: Click **File**, located on the Menu Bar.

Step 4: From the File drop-down menu, select **Print**. The **Print** dialog box will appear with the **General** tab selected.

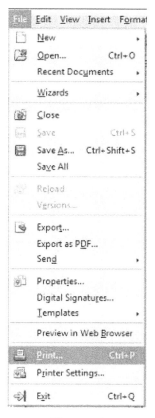

Figure 4

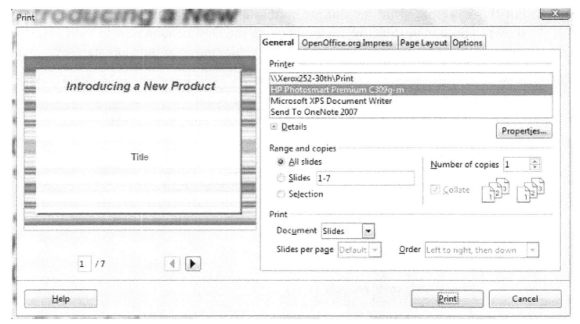

Figure 5

Step 5: From the **Document** drop-down list, select **Outline**. Once Outline has been selected, click **OK**. The outline will be printed.

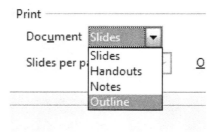

Figure 6

Note – The keyboard shortcut **CTRL + P** will also open the Print dialog box.

Growth & Assessment

1. Users are unable to print an Impress presentation.

    a. TRUE

    b. FALSE

2. What is the keyboard shortcut to access the Print dialog box?

3. Why is it useful to print a presentation?

Section 3.7 – Entering Presenter Notes

Section Objective:

- Learn how to enter Presenter Notes.

Entering Presenter Notes

OpenOffice Impress provides many different tools and features that help its users organize presentations. One of these helpful features is **Presenter Notes**. Presenter Notes are text notes that can be entered into an Impress presentation to help remind the user presenting the slides of the specific information that should be communicated to the audience. Presenter Notes are helpful in all presentations because they help the presenter communicate the information to the audience without having to refer to index cards, or other distracting documentation. The following steps outline how to enter Presenter Notes into an Impress slide.

Step 1: Create a new presentation and select any slide.

   Note – Presenter Notes can be added to any type of slide in OpenOffice Impress.

Step 2: Click **View**, located on the Menu Bar.

Step 3: From the View drop-down menu, check the checkbox next to the **Notes** view. The **Slide Pane** will change and add the **Notes** textbox to the bottom of the selected slide.

   Note – Clicking the **Notes** tab at the top of the **Slide Pane** will also display the Notes textbox.

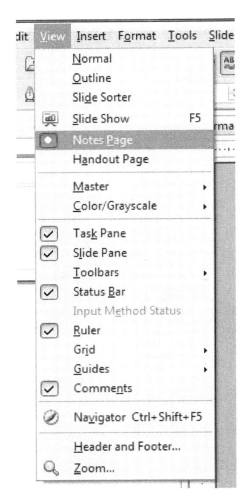

Figure 1

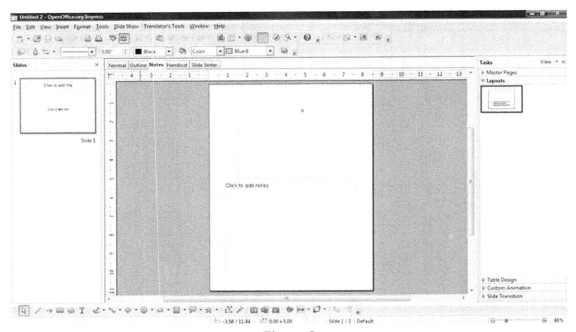

Figure 2

Step 4: Using the left mouse button, click anywhere within the Notes textbox. Enter the necessary presenter notes for the slide and then click outside of the Notes textbox to continue working on the presentation. The presenter notes will remain in the Notes textbox and can be modified at any time.

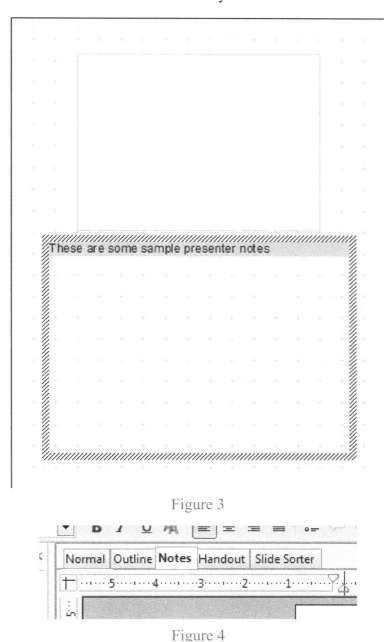

These are some sample presenter notes

Figure 3

| Normal | Outline | Notes | Handout | Slide Sorter |

Figure 4

Note – If a user wants to print the Presenter Notes, they can do so by accessing the Print dialog box and selecting **Notes** from the Document drop-down menu. Once Notes has been selected, click **Print**.

Growth & Assessment

1. The audience is able to see the Presenter Notes.

    a. TRUE

    b. FALSE

2. Aside from accessing the View drop-down menu, how else can a user add Notes?

3. Why are Notes added to a presentation?

Section 3.8 – Changing Font, Size, and Color of Text

Section Objective:

- Learn how to change the font, size, and color of the text.

Changing the Font, Size and Color of the Text

Being able to change the Font, Size, and Color of the text in a presentation is important for many different reasons. One reason is that these modifications allow users to create an eye catching presentation, which is crucial when trying to gain the attention of the audience. Another important reason is that these modifications allow the user to draw attention to specific portions of the presentation, such as important data, or the results of a particular study.

OpenOffice Impress provides two options for accessing the necessary tools to format the text. Users can format the text by using the **Toolbar** icons, or by going through the **Character** dialog box. This section will cover how both of these options can be used to format the text in Impress.

Formatting Text Using the Toolbar

Step 1: Create a new presentation. Within the Title slide textbox, enter the preferred text. After the text has been entered into the textbox, highlight the text.

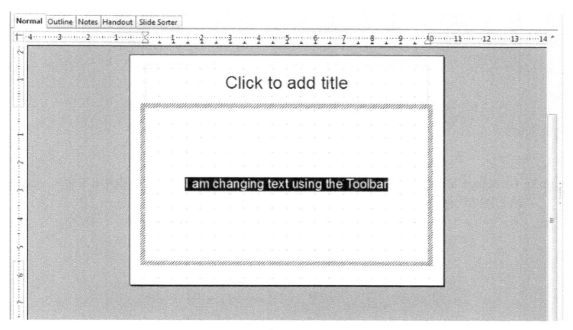

Figure 1

Step 2: From the **Formatting Toolbar**, click the arrow next to the **Font** textbox. A drop-down menu with the available Font options will appear. Select the preferred Font.

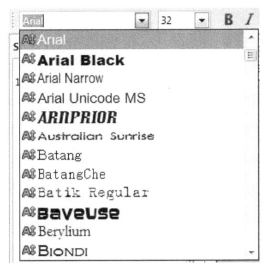

Figure 2

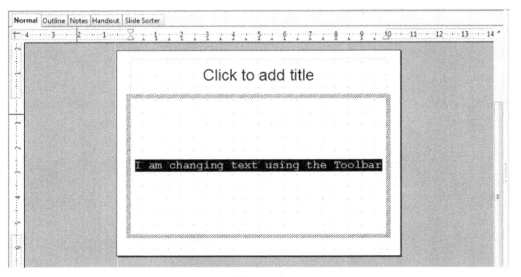

Figure 3

Step 3: To select a different **Font Size**, click on the Font Size pull-down list. Once the available sizes are displayed, select the preferred Font Size.

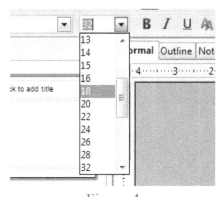

Figure 4

Step 4: To select a different **Font Color**, click the arrow next to **Font Color** and select the preferred color from the options available.

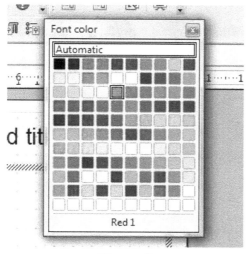

Figure 5

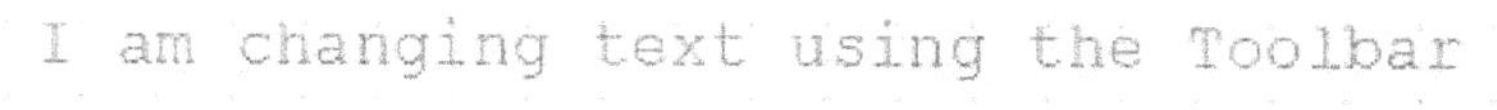

I am changing text using the Toolbar

Figure 6

Formatting Text Using the Character Dialog Box

Step 1: Create a new presentation. Within the Title slide textbox, enter the preferred text. After the text has been entered into the textbox, highlight the text.

Step 2: Click **Format**, located on the Menu Bar.

Step 3: From the Format drop-down menu, click **Character…**. The **Character** dialog box will appear.

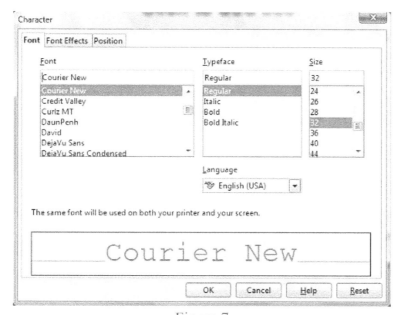

Figure 7

Step 4: Click the **Font** tab located at the top of the Character dialog box.

Step 5: From the **Font** scroll list, select the preferred Font.

Step 6: From the **Size** scroll list, select the preferred Font Size.

Step 7: Click the **Font Effects** tab.

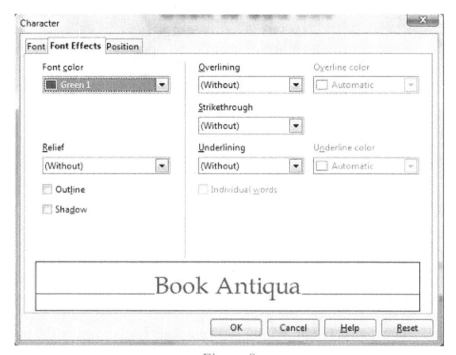

Figure 8

Step 8: In the **Font Color** drop-down menu, select the preferred Font Color.

Step 9: Click **OK**. The changes made in the Character dialog box will be applied to the selected text.

Growth & Assessment

1. What are the two options used to change the Font, Size, and Color of text in a presentation?

2. Changing the Font, Size, and Color of text in a presentation is very important.

    a. TRUE

    b. FALSE

3. What can users change within the Font Effects tab?

Section 3.9 – Changing the Horizontal Alignment of Text

Section Objective:

- Learn how to change the horizontal alignment of text in a slide.

Changing the Horizontal Alignment of the Text

Depending on the style used for an Impress presentation, the horizontal alignment of the text may need to be changed. The application provides users with four different horizontal alignment options which are: Align Left, Centered, Align Right, and Justified. These alignment options can be accessed through the **Format** drop-down menu, by using the **Alignment** buttons located on the **Toolbar**, or by going through the **Quick Menu**. This section will explain how to access the horizontal alignment options by using all three of these methods.

The Format Menu

Step 1: Open a previously created Impress presentation and highlight the text on the first slide.

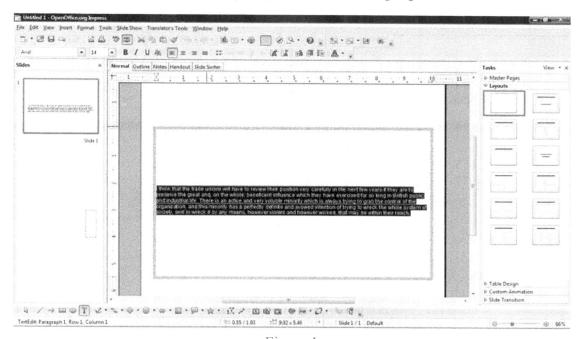

Figure 1

Step 2: Click **Format**, located on the Menu Bar.

Step 3: From the Format drop-down menu, select **Paragraph….** The **Paragraph** dialog box will appear.

Step 4: Click on the **Alignment** tab located at the top of the dialog box. This tab will display the different alignment options available. Click the radio button next to the preferred type of alignment and then click **OK**.

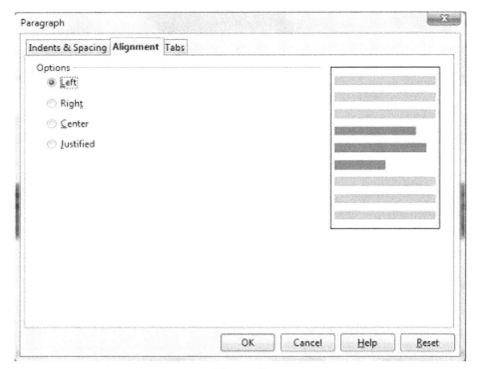

Figure 2

Note – The Paragraph dialog box will display a sample of what the text will look like once a preferred alignment has been selected. Utilize this alignment preview to avoid repeating steps.

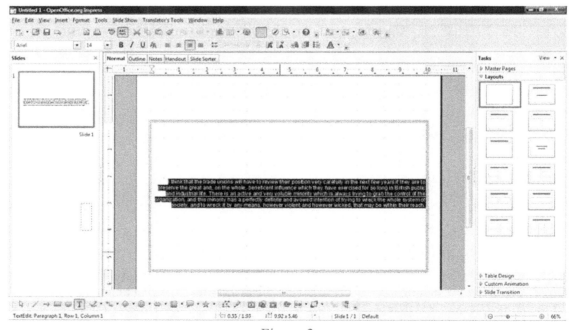

Figure 3

The Alignment buttons, which are located on the Toolbar, allow users to quickly adjust the horizontal alignment while working on a presentation. Refer to the figure below to identify the type of horizontal alignment that corresponds with each button.

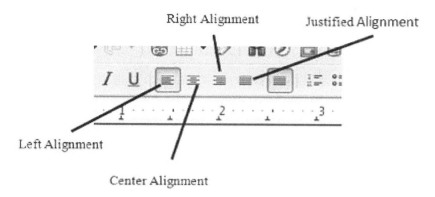

Figure 4

The Quick Menu

As stated above, Impress allows users to change the horizontal alignment by going through the **Quick Menu**. This can be done by following the steps below.

Step 1: Open a previously created Impress presentation and highlight the text on the first slide.

Step 2: Right-click on the selected text. The Quick Menu will appear.

Step 3: From the Quick Menu, select the preferred alignment for the selected text.

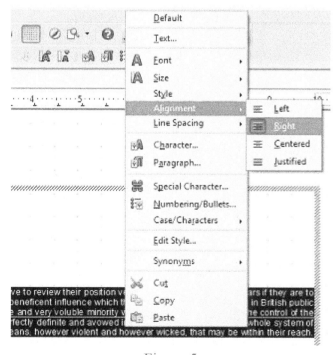

Figure 5

Growth & Assessment

1. How many horizontal alignment options are available?

2. List the different ways to change the horizontal alignment of text.

3. OpenOffice Impress allows its users to change the horizontal text alignment in a presentations.

   a. TRUE

   b. FALSE

4. What are the alignment options?

Section 3.10 – Adjusting the Spacing in a Slide

Section Objective:

- Learn how to adjust the text spacing in a slide.

Adjust the Spacing in a Slide

OpenOffice Impress allows users to change the spacing between lines of text in a slide. This is helpful when manipulating the text to fit a defined area within the slide. It is also useful when a user needs to make the text easier to read. The following steps outline how this is done in OpenOffice Impress.

Note – The default spacing in OpenOffice Impress is 1.0.

Step 1: Create a new Impress presentation and add a slide with a Blank Layout.

Step 2: On the blank slide, create a textbox and enter the preferred text.

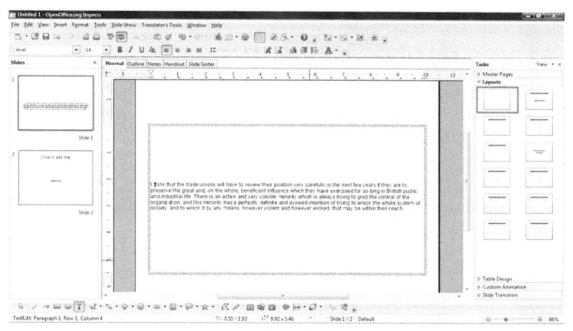

Figure 1

Step 3: Click **Format**, located on the Menu Bar.

Step 4: From the Format drop-down menu, select **Paragraph…**. The **Paragraph** dialog box will appear with the **Indents & Spacing** tab selected.

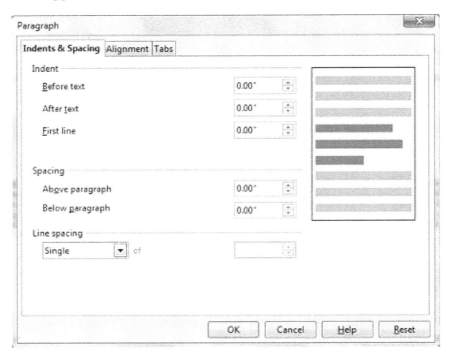

Figure 2

Step 5: From the **Line Spacing** portion of the dialog box, the user has the ability to select the desired line spacing from the drop-down menu. The spacing options available are listed below.

Line Spacing Options:

- Single

- 1.5 Lines

- Double

- Proportional

- At Least

- Leading

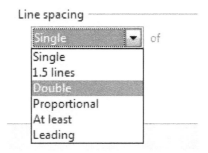

Figure 3

Step 6: After selecting the preferred spacing, click **OK**. The new spacing will be added to the slide.

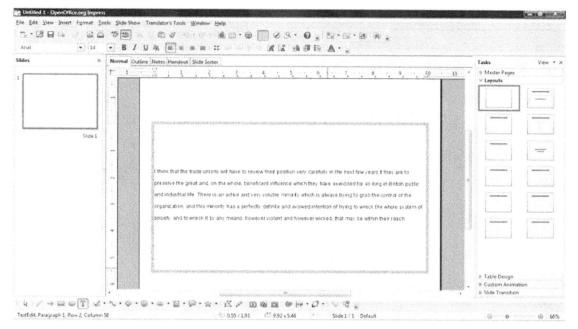

Figure 4

Impress also allows users to adjust the amount of blank space that is displayed before and after paragraphs. The following steps outline how this is done.

Note – For the purpose of this example, use the same presentation and textbox as used in the steps above.

Step 1: Click **Format**, located on the Menu Bar.

Step 2: From the Format drop-down menu, select **Paragraph…**. The Paragraph dialog box will appear with the **Indents & Spacing** tab selected.

Step 3: From the **Spacing** portion of the dialog box, use the arrows or manually enter the values for the preferred spacing in both the **Above Paragraph** and **Below** Paragraph fields.

Figure 5

Step 4: Click **OK**. The selected width will be inserted between the paragraphs on the slide.

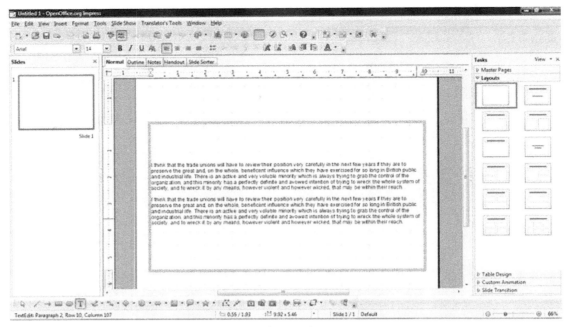

Figure 6

Growth & Assessment

1. What is the default line spacing?

2. Users are unable to change line spacing in Impress.

    a. TRUE

    b. FALSE

3. Why is changing the line spacing useful?

Section 3.11 – Adding Transitions to Slides

Section Objective:

- Learn how to add transitions to slides.

Adding Transitions

OpenOffice Impress allows users to choose from a variety of Transitions. Transitions are used in presentations to add an artistic flare when one slide gives way to the next. Transitions are typically combinations of animation and sound, and can be added through the Slide Transition task pane. The following steps explain how a user can apply Transitions to a presentation.

Step 1: Create a new Impress presentation that contains at least two slides. Enter different text into each slide so they both contain different information.

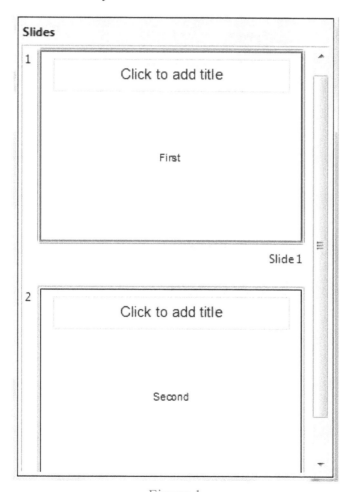

Figure 1

Step 2: Click **Slide Show**, located on the Menu Bar.

Step 3: Within the Slide Show drop-down menu, select **Slide Transition…**. The **Slide Transition** task pane will appear on the right side of the Impress window.

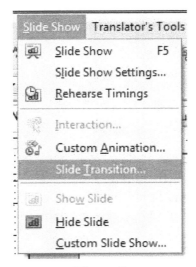

Figure 2

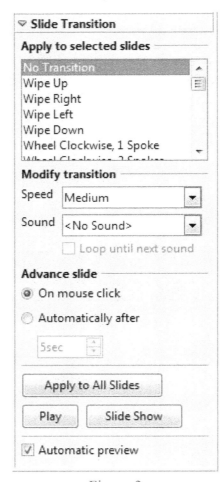

Figure 3

Step 4: The list of available transitions can be viewed by scrolling through the selection box at the top of the Slide Transition task pane. Select different transitions and view a preview of their action in the Slide pane, located in the middle of the Impress window. For this particular example, select the **Cover Down** transition. Once the transition has been selected, the preview will be displayed in the Slide pane.

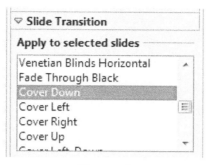

Figure 4

Step 5: Select the preferred speed of the transition from the **Speed** pull-down list. For this example, select **Medium**.

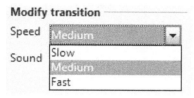

Figure 5

Step 6: A sound can also be added to the transition by going to the **Sound** pull-down list. For this example, select the **Applause** sound.

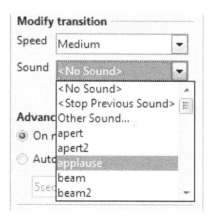

Figure 6

Note – To apply the transition to all of the presentation's slides, click **Apply to All Slides**.

Figure 7

Deleting Transitions

As with other options in Impress, if a transition is no longer needed, it can be removed. The following steps outline how this is done.

Step 1: Select the slide with the transition that is to be deleted. For this example, select the first slide.

Step 2: Select **Slide Show**, located on the Menu Bar.

Step 3: Within the Slide Show drop-down menu, select **Slide Transition....** The **Slide Transition** task pane will appear on the right side of the Impress window.

Step 4: Within the same selection box where the previous transition was chosen, select **No Transition**.

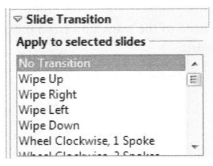

Figure 8

Note – To delete the transition from all of the presentation's slides, click **Apply to All Slides**.

Growth & Assessment

1. Transitions are typically combinations of animation and sound.

    a. TRUE

    b. FALSE

2. Why are transitions used?

3. OpenOffice Impress allows the user to choose from a wide array of transitions.

    a. TRUE

    b. FALSE

Section 3.12 – Adding Slide Timings

Section Objective:

- Learn how to add slide timings.

Adding Slide Timings

OpenOffice Impress allows users to control the amount of time a slide remains on the screen before moving to the next slide. This feature is referred to as slide timing. Impress offers several ways to adjust slide timing, which is explained in the steps below.

Step 1: Create a new Impress presentation and add a blank slide after the Title slide. Select the Title slide.

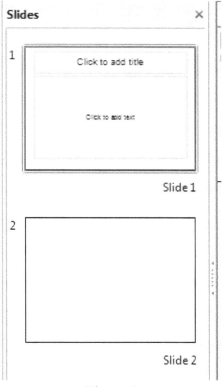

Figure 1

Step 2: Click **Slide Show**, located on the Menu Bar.

Step 3: From the Slide Show drop-down menu, select **Slide Transition…**. The **Slide Transition** task pane will appear along the right side of the Impress window.

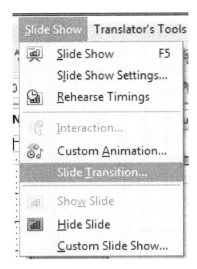

Figure 2

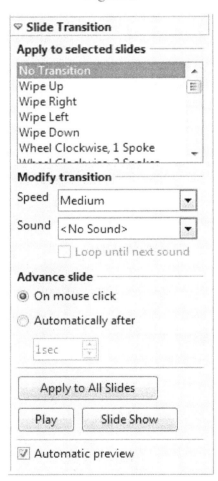

Figure 3

Step 4: Within the **Advance Slide** portion of the task pane, click the radio button next to **Automatically After**. Once clicked, the textbox below the radio button will become available for modification. Use the nudge buttons to select the desired time. For this example, set the transition time to **5**.

Figure 4

Note – Impress allows users to manually advance the slides by hitting the spacebar, even if the slide timing has been applied to the transition.

Step 5: Apply the slide timing to all of the slides in the presentation by clicking **Apply to All Slides**.

Figure 5

Removing Slide Timings

OpenOffice Impress allows users to remove the slide timing if it is no longer needed. The following steps outline how this is done.

Step 1: Select the Title slide and right-click. This will cause the Quick Menu to appear.

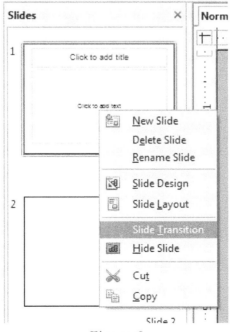

Figure 6

Step 2: From the Quick Menu, select **Slide Transition**. The Slide Transition task pane will open.

Step 3: Within the **Advance Slide** portion of the task pane, click the radio button next to **On Mouse Click**. This will remove the set timings of the slide, and will only advance when the user presses the spacebar.

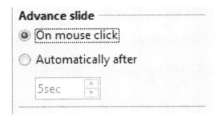

Figure 7

Growth & Assessment

1. Users are able to manually advance the slides by hitting the spacebar even if there is a slide timing set.

    a. TRUE

    b. FALSE

2. During a slide presentation, a slide must remain on the screen for three seconds.

    a. TRUE

    b. FALSE

3. What is slide timing?

4. What task pane is accessed to set slide timing?

Section 3.13 – Embedding and Linking Objects

Section Objective:

- Learn how to embed and link objects.

Embedding and Linking Objects

There may be times when a user needs to embed an existing document, or the link to an existing document, into a slide. This document will then be accessed during the slide presentation. OpenOffice Impress allows the user to embed objects and links using an OLE object, or Object Linking and Embedding object. If an object is embedded, the user can double-click the object and it will appear in the presentation. If the user is linking an object rather than embedding one, a small icon will be displayed in the slide which can be clicked to access the linked object. This section will explain how a user can utilize both of these features in an Impress presentation.

Embedding an OLE Object

Step 1: Create a new presentation and click in the content portion of the Title slide.

Step 2: Click **Insert**, located on the Menu Bar.

Step 3: From the Insert drop-down menu, select **Object** and then click **OLE Object**. The **Insert OLE Object** dialog box will appear on the screen.

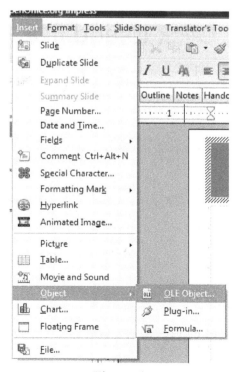

Figure 1

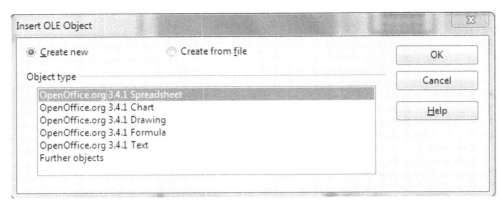

Figure 2

Step 4: Click the radio button next to **Create New** and then select the type of file to embed from the available options. For this example, select **OpenOffice.org 3.4.1 Spreadsheet**.

Object type

OpenOffice.org 3.4.1 Spreadsheet
OpenOffice.org 3.4.1 Chart
OpenOffice.org 3.4.1 Drawing
OpenOffice.org 3.4.1 Formula
OpenOffice.org 3.4.1 Text
Further objects

Figure 3

Step 5: Click **OK**. An empty spreadsheet will be added to the slide.

Figure 4

Note – The spreadsheet can be worked on as if it were a regular OpenOffice Calc spreadsheet.

Step 1: Click **Insert**, located on the Menu Bar.

Step 2: From the Insert drop-down menu, select **Object** and then click **OLE Object**. The **Insert OLE Object** dialog box will appear on the screen.

Step 3: Click the radio button next to **Create from File**. The dialog box will automatically change to look like the figure below.

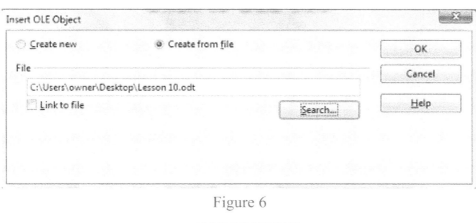

Figure 5

Step 4: Click on the **Search** button to access the **Open** dialog box. Search through saved files and find an OpenOffice Writer or Calc document to link to the presentation. Once the desired file has been selected, click the **Open** button. Click the checkbox next to **Link to file**.

Figure 6

Figure 7

Step 5: Click **OK**. The file selected will be linked to the presentation and the object icon will be inserted into the presentation.

    Note – Once a link has been created between the two files, any modifications to the files will be shown when the object icon is clicked. This means that if a user makes any changes to the linked Writer or Calc file, the changes will be reflected in the Impress presentation and vice versa.

Growth & Assessment

1. What does OLE stand for?

2. How would a user access an embedded object?

3. Linking an object rather than embedding it will save space on the slide by using a small icon to represent the object.

   a. TRUE

   b. FALSE

Section 3.14 – Exporting a Presentation into PDF

Section Objective:

- Learn how export a presentation into PDF.

Exporting to a PDF

OpenOffice Impress allows users export any presentation to the PDF file type. PDF stands for Portable Document Format and it is industry-standard file format for file viewing. A PDF is ideal when sending the file to someone because, regardless of what type of software is installed on the recipient's computer, they will be able to load the PDF file.

Impress provides two ways of exporting a presentation to a PDF. This first set of steps will outline how a user can export directly to a PDF, while having Impress make all the formatting decisions automatically.

Step 1: Create a new Impress presentation.

Step 2: Click the **Export to PDF** button found on the **Toolbar**.

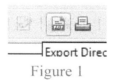

Figure 1

Step 3: The **Export** dialog will appear on the screen. Here, the user has the ability to enter the file name and select the save location for the exported file. Enter the preferred file name and select a destination folder for the exported presentation.

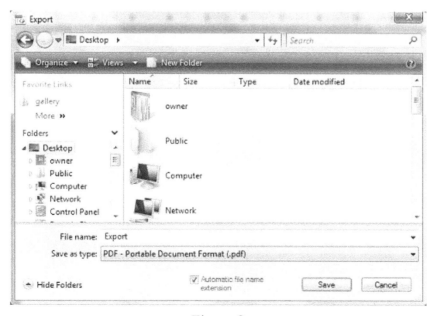

Figure 2

Step 4: Once the file name and export destination have been specified in the Export dialog box, click **Save**. The presentation will be exported to a PDF file.

Figure 3

The second way of exporting to a PDF is to navigate through the **File** drop-down menu and use the **PDF Options** dialog box to modify the specifics of the exported file. The next portion of this section will go through the steps to do this, as well as provide the user with information about the different modifications that can be made in the PDF Options dialog box.

Step 1: Using the same Impress file that was used in the steps above, click the **File**, on the Menu Bar.

Step 2: From the File drop-down menu, select **Export as PDF…**. The **PDF Options** dialog box will appear with the **General** tab selected.

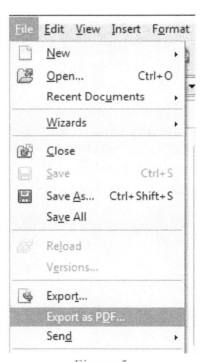

Figure 5

Step 3: Within the General tab, the user has the ability to specify which pages to include in the PDF, select the type of compression to use for images (this will affect the size, and the quality of the pictures), as well as other options. Select the preferred options and then click the **Initial View** tab.

Figure 6

Step 4: Within the Initial View tab, the user has the ability to select how the PDF will open in the PDF reader. The PDF reader is the software used by computers to open PDF files. Select the preferred options and then click the **User Interface** tab.

> **Note** – In most situations, the options in the Initial View tab should be left at their default value.

Figure 7

Step 5: Within the User Interface tab, the user has the ability to modify more settings to control how a PDF reader displays the exported presentation. Make the desired modifications and then click the **Links** tab.

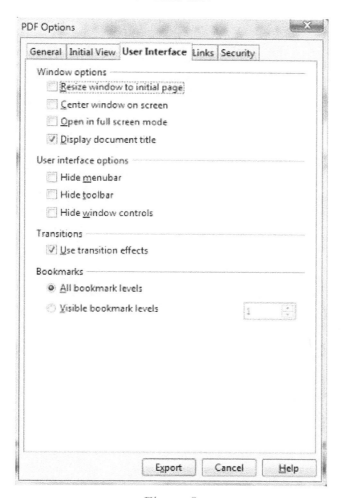

Figure 8

Step 6: Within the Links tab, the user can choose how to manage any links between the exported PDF file and the original Impress presentation file. This screen will be used very infrequently; however, if modifications are desired, do so and then click the **Security** tab.

Figure 9

Step 7: Within the Security tab, the user has the option to make the exported presentation password protected. If this option is selected, the pane will offer additional fields where the user can set restrictions for other actions performed on the exported presentation. Once the desired selections have been made, click the **Export** button. The **Export** dialog box will appear.

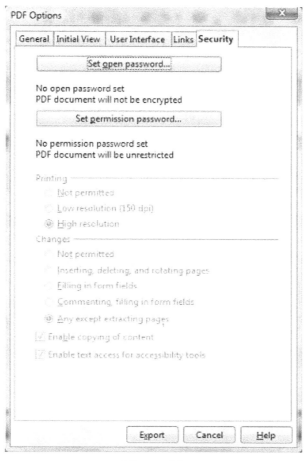

Figure 10

Step 8: Within the Export dialog box, the user has the ability to enter the file name and select a save location for the exported file. Enter the preferred file name and select a destination folder for the exported presentation.

Step 9: Once the file name and export destination have been specified in the Export dialog box, click **Save**. The presentation will be exported to a PDF file.

Growth & Assessment

1. PDF stands for "Possible Document File."

    a. TRUE

    b. FALSE

2. What is the industry-standard file format?

3. What does PDF stand for?

4. How many ways can users export a presentation as a PDF?

Section 3.15 – Showing a Presentation

Section Objective:

- Learn how to show a presentation.

Showing a Presentation

An OpenOffice Impress presentation is designed to present information in an organized and visually appealing way. All parts of the presentations should move and transition cleanly allowing the audience to easily follow along. The following steps explain how a user can show a completed presentation.

Starting the Slide Show

Step 1: Open Impress and create a new presentation.

Step 2: Select the desired Template for the presentation.

Step 3: Click **Slide Show**, located on the Menu Bar.

Step 4: From the Slide Show drop-down menu, click **Slide Show**. Once the Slide Show option has been clicked, the Slide Show will begin automatically.

Different Ways of Starting the Slide Show

Impress provides multiple ways of starting the Slide Show. View the various starting options listed below.

Starting Options:

- **View Menu** – Click **View Slide Show**

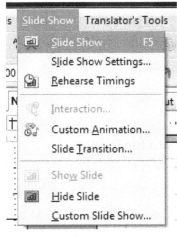

Figure 1

- **Slide Show Button** – Click the Slide Show button located on the right side of the Toolbar.

Figure 2

- **Keyboard Shortcut** – Press **F5**

- **Advance to the Next Slide** – If Slide Timings have not been set up for the presentation, Impress allows users to press the spacebar to advance from one slide to the next. Users can also use the left and right arrows to move forward and backwards through the slides.

- **End the Slide Show** – Impress allows users to end the Slide Show at any time by pressing the **ESC** key.

Growth & Assessment

1. How does a user end a slide show?

2. The Slide Show feature can be accessed through the Menu Bar.

   a. TRUE

   b. FALSE

3. What button, from the Toolbar, can be selected to begin a slide show?

Appendix

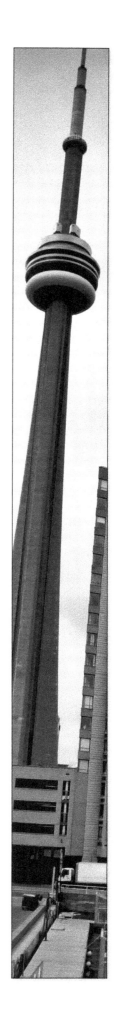

OpenOffice Volume IV: Impress Unit 1

Section 1.1

1. ClipArt is a picture that can be added to a presentation.

2. A Wizard is a step-by-step guide for completing a task in Impress.

3. a. TRUE

4. A Master contains formatting and design elements common to every slide in a presentation.

Section 1.2

1. a. TRUE

2. Position the cursor over the icon and the tool's name will automatically appear on the screen.

3. a. TRUE

Section 1.3

1. b. FALSE

2. Vertical orientation

3. a. TRUE

4. Changing the orientation is important when the user needs to accommodate a particular style or illustration within a slide.

Section 1.4

1. CTRL + X

2. b. FALSE

3. CTRL + V

Section 1.5

1. Normal view is the main editing view. Here, the user can write and design the presentation.

2. Five choices

3. a. TRUE

4. It allows the user to type notes in the Notes pane, which is located just below the Slide pane in Normal view.

Section 1.6

1. The Ruler option allows the user to set, move, delete, or change tabs while working on a slide.

2. Left, Right, Center, and Decimal

3. a. TRUE

Section 1.7

1. The Help button

2. a. TRUE

3. A small question mark

Section 1.8

1. a. TRUE

2. A blank Title slide

3. This is convenient because it allows the user to start creating a new presentation as soon as the application opens.

Section 1.9

1. b. FALSE

2. Presentations with a pre-designed slide format

3. As a starting point for an Impress presentation

4. Any of the following: Business proposals, technical specs, product descriptions

Section 1.10

1. To delete the textbox, select the border of the textbox so that it is highlighted. Then press DELETE. The textbox will be deleted from the slide.

2. The T

3. a. TRUE

4. b. FALSE

Section 1.11

1. b. FALSE

2. Layouts found within the Tasks pane

3. b. FALSE

Section 1.12

1. CTRL + S

2. .odp

3. a. TRUE

Section 1.13

1. Consistency adds credibility as well as organization to a presentation.

2. By using the Slide Master

3. a. TRUE

Section 1.14

1. a. TRUE

2. b. FALSE

3. A theme is a particular style that uses colors, textures, and font styles.

Section 1.15

1. The Find tool allows the user to quickly locate particular text within a document.

2. a. TRUE

3. a. TRUE

4. Replaces all occurrences of one word with the new word

OpenOffice Volume IV: Impress Unit 2

Section 2.1

1. By using the Quick Menu

2. a. TRUE

3. On the Menu bar, click on Tools and then select Spelling

4. The Spelling dialog box includes the Ignore Once, Change, and Change All options.

Section 2.2

1. The user can include a logo or emblem on each page of the handouts

2. a. FALSE

3. The Handout page is located under the View menu.

4. a. TRUE

Section 2.3

1. From the OpenOffice.org Impress tab the user is able to select any special fields to be included on the print out such as the file name, date, and any hidden pages.

2. a. TRUE

3. To print specific slides the user can separate a non-sequential range using commas.

4. 2-4, 6, 12, 14-16, 20-21, 25

Section 2.4

1. a. FALSE

2. The user can use the Fontwork Gallery to make the text in the document more eye-catching. Text created through the Fontwork Gallery can be resized and edited to fit the user's needs.

3. If the Drawing Toolbar isn't visible on the screen, go to View > Toolbars > Drawing to make it visible.

4. From the Tools menu, click Gallery

Section 2.5

1. Having them in the same directory or folder as the Impress presentation will eliminate the need to link them

2. OpenOffice Impress does not come preloaded with any GIFs.

3. Click on the Insert menu on the Menu bar. From the expanded Insert menu select Movie and Sound.

4. a. TRUE

Section 2.6

1. Animation refers to the movement and sound accompanying text or slides in a presentation.

2. Objects that can be animated include: images, charts, and text.

3. a. TRUE

4. In the Speed drop-down users are able to choose the speed at which the animation occurs

Section 2.7

1. a. TRUE

2. b. FALSE

3. Users can use the Custom Animation pane to control the order of the animations.

4. Users can validate that the animations added to the slides work at any time by clicking Play at the bottom of the Custom Animation task pane.

Section 2.8

1. Impress will automatically insert a three-bar Column Chart as the default chart.

2. b. False

3. Right-click anywhere in the chart area and select Chart Type….

4. Right-click anywhere in the chart area and select Chart Data Table….

Section 2.9

1. The Borders tab allows the user to set the style and width of the border that will be used in the chart.

2. The Area tab allows the user to set the type of background fill that will be shown for the chart.

3. The Transparency tab lets the user change the background of the chart by either making the background have a level of transparency or by implementing a Gradient.

4. a. TRUE

Section 2.10

1. Tables in OpenOffice Impress are very useful and versatile for arranging text into columns and rows within the slides.

2. b. FALSE

3. Choose the number of Columns and Rows to be inserted into the table from the Size portion of the dialog box.

4. The Drag Method is a way to quickly insert blank tables into presentations.

Section 2.11

1. a. TRUE

2. Duplicate Slide is found under the Insert menu on the Menu bar.

3. An exact duplicate, with all of the formatting and content from the original slide, will be inserted directly below the slide currently selected.

4. Click and hold the left mouse button on the chosen slide, drag it, and then release the mouse button.

Section 2.12

1. There will be times that the user will be able to save time when creating an Impress presentation by re-using slides from previous presentations.

2. a. TRUE

3. From the expanded Insert menu, select File....

4. The slide(s) the user selected will be placed underneath the currently selected slide in the presentation.

Section 2.13

1. Interactions allow the user to assign links to button shapes that have been added to the presentation, and then assign them an action that will occur upon the click of a mouse.

2. A target sound file containing the sound to be played

3. a. TRUE

4. The Action at Mouse Click drop-down menu lets the user choose the action that takes place.

Section 2.14

1. Users can add both slide numbers and the date and time into the slides.

2. The Slide Number checkbox is found on the Slide tab of Headers and Footers dialog box.

3. b. FALSE

4. a. TRUE

Section 2.15

1. Grayscale has different hues of gray for different parts of the slide.

2. Users can select Color/Grayscale by clicking on the View menu from the Menu bar.

3. b. FALSE

4. b. FALSE

OpenOffice Volume IV: Impress Unit 3

Section 3.1

1. Allows the user to use a picture as the background

2. a. TRUE

3. To make a presentation more visually appealing and to appeal to different audiences

Section 3.2

1. a. TRUE

2. Four

3. Color, gradient, hatching, bitmap

4. Hatches are a series of lines. They will run vertical, horizontal, and diagonal in a series of patterns.

Section 3.3

1. In the Format menu

2. a. TRUE

3. Basic gradients, and basic textures

Section 3.4

1. a. TRUE

2. The main title heading for the slide will be displayed

3. It will cause all of the sub headings to reappear.

Section 3.5

1. a. TRUE

2. Moving the text up or down the slide or to a new slide.

3. The Toolbar

Section 3.6

1. b. FALSE

2. CTRL + P

3. It allows the audience to have a physical copy of the presentation to follow along with during the digital showing of the presentation.

Section 3.7

1. a. TRUE

2. Clicking the Notes tab at the top of the Slide Pane

3. To give the presenter clues about the slide

Section 3.8

1. Using the Toolbar icons or through the Font dialog box

2. a. TRUE

3. The color

Section 3.9

1. Three

2. Alignment options for text can be accessed through the Format menu from the Menu bar, by using the Alignment buttons on the Toolbar, or by using the Quick Menu.

3. a. TRUE

4. Align Left, Centered, Align Right, and Justified

Section 3.10

1. 1.0

2. b. FALSE

3. It is a useful feature to use when the user needs to make the text easier to read

Section 3.11

1. a. TRUE

2. Transitions are used in presentations to add an artistic flare when one slide gives way to the next.

3. a. TRUE

Section 3.12

1. a. TRUE

2. b. FALSE

3. The amount of time a slide remains on the screen.

4. Slide Transitions task pane

Section 3.13

1. Object Linking and Embedding

2. Double-clicking the object

3. a. TRUE

Section 3.14

1. b. FALSE

2. PDF

3. Portable Document Format

4. Two

Section 3.15

1. By pressing the ESC key or F5

2. a. TRUE

3. The Slide Show button